趣味識字
Fun with Chinese
A Chinese Character Learning Curriculum

第十五冊
Workbook 15

自序

我是一位在美國的自學媽媽，孩子的中文學習完全由我親自教導。

在傳統教學方式的薰陶下許多家長認為孩子學中文必須先從注音開始，往往也認為中文字筆畫眾多複雜對小孩來說太難。其實對幼兒來說每一個中文字都只是一個圖案，幼兒的記憶力非常強，認字對他們來說並不困難。

我自己的兩個孩子都是從認字開始學習中文的。當初我會設計趣味識字是因為在市面上並沒有找到令我完全滿意的教材，絕大多數的教材都是從注音符號或是筆畫簡單的字開始教學。雖然筆劃較少容易書寫但往往這些字在日常生活上並不常見，在孩子的世界裡更是沒有應用的機會。而市面上認字的教材卻普遍地缺乏動手的參與感。孩子在學習的過程中常常覺得教材枯燥乏味，既沒趣味又缺乏實用性。這樣的學習對孩子來說不但痛苦也沒有效率。使用這些教材後我發現自己一直在動手製作輔助教材來提昇孩子的學習興趣。

我一直深信一定要讓孩子覺得有趣和實用，他們才會有學習的動力，有了動力才會學得好。所以趣味識字的設計是以先教常用字的方式讓孩子能夠快速進入閱讀，因而發覺識字的實用性。當孩子懂得如何應用文字後，學習自信自然就提高了。製作輔助教材時為了幫助孩子加強對生字的記憶，除了使用字卡和遊戲的方式複習，我也設計了一系列的遊戲習題，而這些習題就是趣味識字誕生的前奏。

最後非常感謝您選擇趣味識字做為孩子的教材，也希望這套教材可以幫助您的孩子快樂學習中文。

Preface

I am a homeschooling mom in America who successfully taught my two children to read Chinese at a young age.

Many people think that learning Chinese must start with pinyin because Chinese characters are too complicated and believed to be too difficult for children. However, in children's minds, each Chinese character is just like a picture and memorization is not difficult for them.

Both my children learned to read Chinese beginning with character recognition, yet the process was not easy for me. Existing textbooks often start teaching with pinyin or start with rarely used characters with minimal strokes for writing. Books that emphasize character recognition also tend to be less interactive and less hands-on causing the learning process to be tedious and unmotivating for children. I found myself constantly needing to create my own teaching materials while using these textbooks; and this is the reason for the creation of Fun with Chinese.

Fun with Chinese is designed to teach the most commonly used Chinese characters first, quickly allowing children to be able to read meaningful phrases and sentences from the very beginning. Pictures and games are also used to help with character retention, and each lesson includes reading passages to review previously learned characters.

Today, I am sharing with you this wonderful system that I have used with my own children and hoping to make your child's Chinese learning an easy and enjoyable journey.

— Anchia Tai

關於英文翻譯

習題本中的句子都有中英雙語，希望讓中文不是很好的家長們也有辦法使用教材。其中朗讀句子練習中的英文翻譯也盡量讓句型和中文相對應幫助英文為母語的家長容易理解。

About the English Translations

The English translations in the workbooks are specifically designed in a way to closely match up with the Chinese sentence grammar structure. While this might make the translations grammatically incorrect in English, the design will help English speakers to learn and understand the Chinese sentences better.

關於筆順

本書中的國字筆順是依據中華民國教育部「常用國字標準字體筆順學習網」的筆劃順序彙編。中華民國教育部對於部分筆順有做調整，可能於傳統書寫筆順有所差異，不同華人地區的筆順也可能有所不同。如果本書中的筆順與家長所學的筆順有所差異，請自行調整教學。

About the Stroke Orders

The stroke orders of the characters in this workbook follow the stroke orders provided on the "Learning Program for Stroke Order of Frequently Used Chinese Characters" website of the Ministry of Education, R.O.C. (Taiwan). The authors are aware that there were changes to the stroke orders made by the Ministry of Education as well as regional differences in character stroke orders. Please feel free to make adjustments in teaching if the stroke orders are different in your region.

每當完成一課後請回到本頁將該課的花朵塗上顏色。
Please color a flower after you have completed a lesson.

1

相 業 它 呢
者 之 賣 題 難
片 名 許 目 右
            左
入 應 該 清 安
石 加 法 讓 喜

第一課

Lesson 1 Xiāng – each other; one another; mutually
Xiàng – appearance; picture; government minister

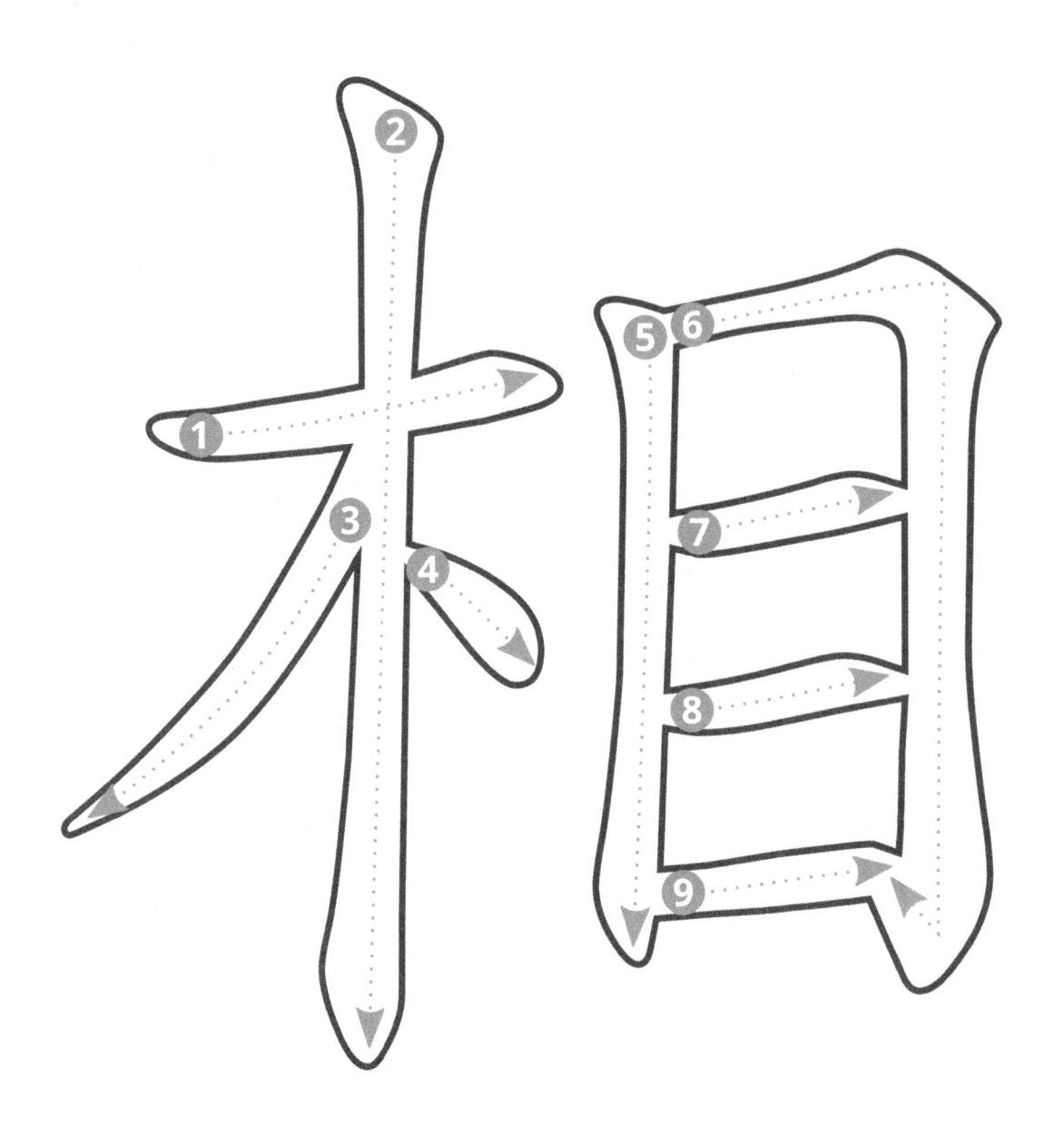

本書中的國字筆順是依據中華民國教育部「常用國字標準字體筆順學習網」的筆劃順序彙編。
The stroke orders of the characters in this workbook follow the stroke orders provided on the "Learning Program for Stroke Order of Frequently Used Chinese Characters" website of the Ministry of Education, R.O.C. (Taiwan).

將有「相」字的澆水器著色。
Color the watering cans with the character 相.

4

唸出下面的語詞。
Read aloud the phrases below.

相信

長相

相機

相愛

唸唸看
Read-Aloud

- 今天學校門口來了一個我沒有見過的男人。

  A man I've never seen before shows up today at the school's entrance.

- 他問我可不可以幫他找走失的小狗。

  He asks me if I can help him find his lost puppy.

- 姑姑和我說過不可以相信沒見過的人。

  (My) aunt tells me to not trust anyone that I've not seen before.

- 而且大人也不會找小孩子幫忙。

  Besides, adults also will not find kids to help (them).

- 任何人都有可能是壞人,我不可以相信他。

  Anyone can be a bad person, I cannot trust him.

恭喜你完成了這一課,請回到第一頁將本課的花朵塗上顏色。
Congratulations! You have completed a lesson. Please color the flower for this lesson on page 1.

第二課

Lesson 2 Zhě – (after a verb or adjective) one who (is) ...; (after a noun) person involved in ...; -er; -ist

本書中的國字筆順是依據中華民國教育部「常用國字標準字體筆順學習網」的筆劃順序彙編。
The stroke orders of the characters in this workbook follow the stroke orders provided on the "Learning Program for Stroke Order of Frequently Used Chinese Characters" website of the Ministry of Education, R.O.C. (Taiwan).

找出「者」字圈出來。
Find the characters 者 and circle them.

堵　　　　　　　都

　　　　者

著　　　　　　老

　　　堵　　　　者

者

　　　者

跟著「者」字從 ➡ 到 ★ 走出迷宮。
Follow the characters 者 from the arrow to the star to exit the maze.

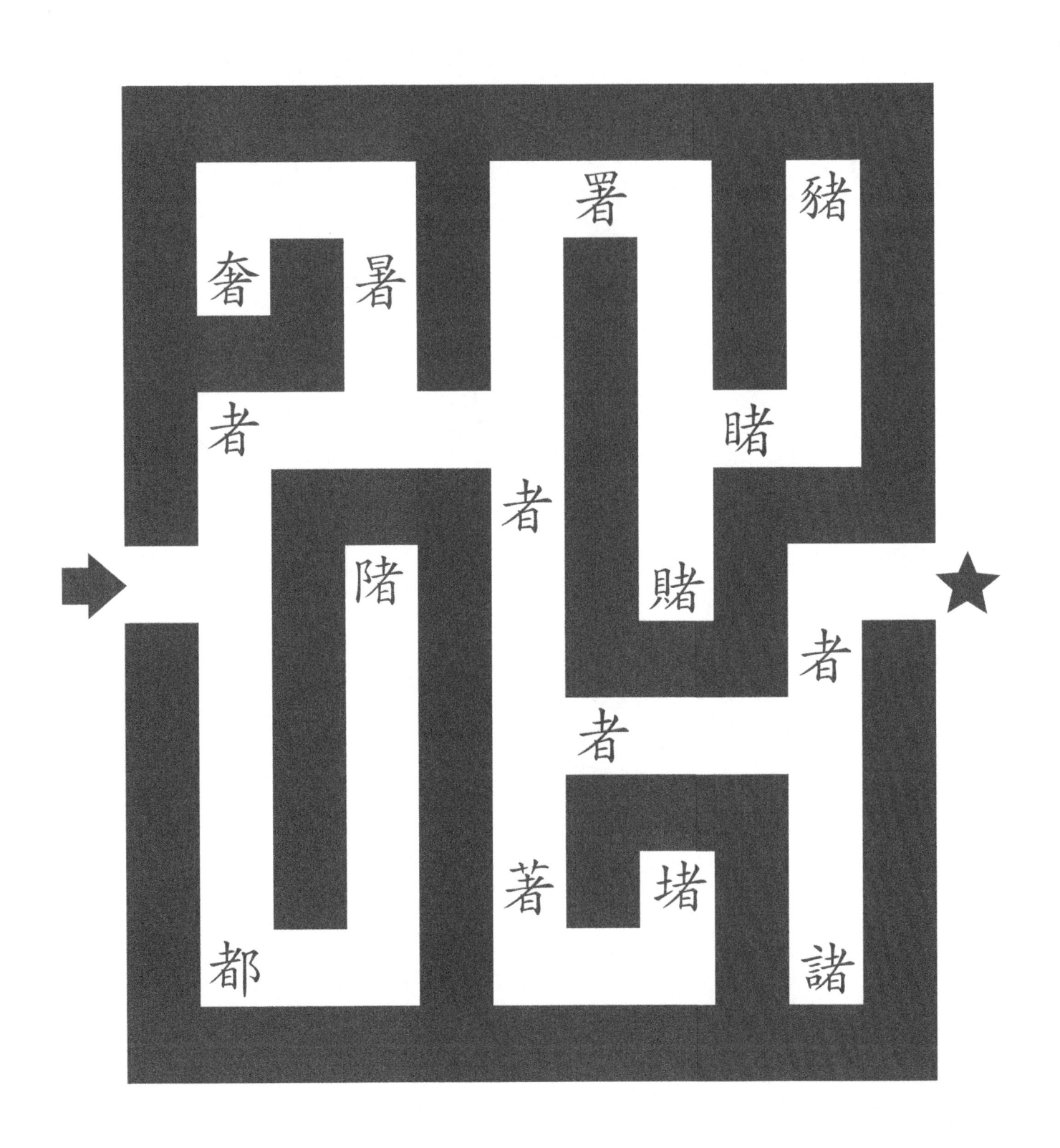

唸唸看
Read-Aloud

- 我長大以後想要當記者。
  When I grow up, I want to be a reporter.

- 因為這樣就可以經常上電視。
  Because (I) can often be on T.V.

- 媽媽說記者的中文要很好。
  Mom says a reporter's Chinese has to be good.

- 我相信我可以完成任何的夢想。
  I believe I can achieve any dream.

- 我要每天用功學好中文。
  I am going to study Chinese well everyday.

恭喜你完成了這一課,請回到第一頁將本課的花朵塗上顏色。
Congratulations! You have completed a lesson. Please color the flower for this lesson on page 1.

第三課

Lesson 3 Piàn – classifier for slices, tablets, tract of land, area of water; film; partial

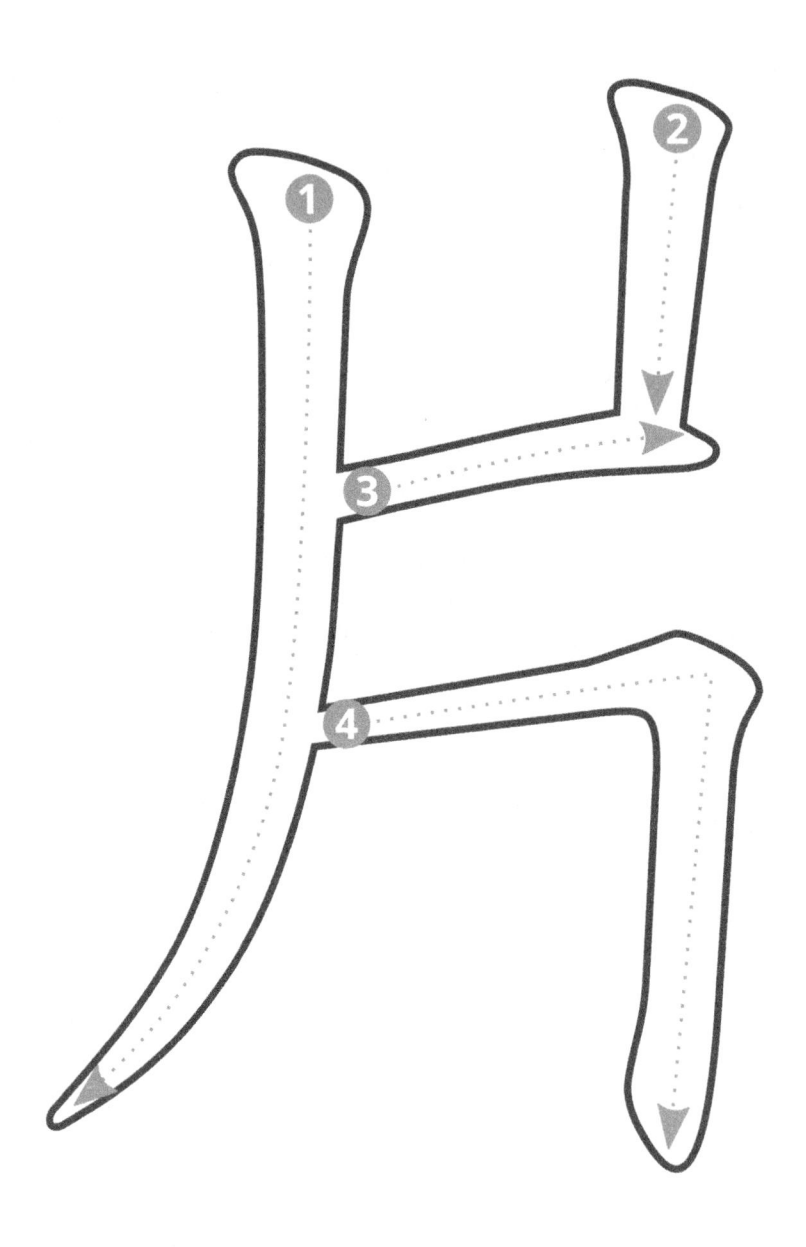

本書中的國字筆順是依據中華民國教育部「常用國字標準字體筆順學習網」的筆劃順序彙編。
The stroke orders of the characters in this workbook follow the stroke orders provided on the "Learning Program for Stroke Order of Frequently Used Chinese Characters" website of the Ministry of Education, R.O.C. (Taiwan).

請圈出正確的數量。
Please circle the correct quantities.

三片／一片

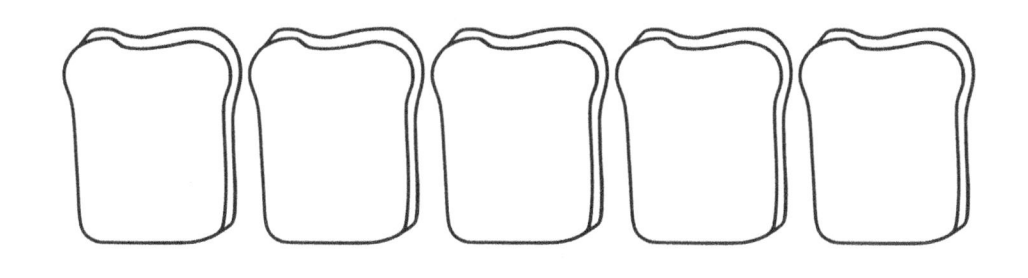

三片／兩片

四片／五片

一片／五片

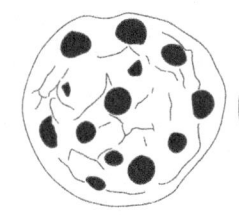

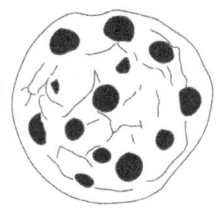

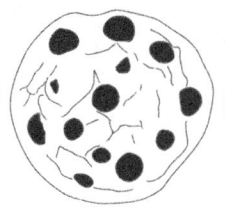

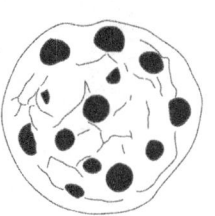

四片／三片

12

請在下框中貼上一張你喜歡的相片並唸出下面的文字。
Please paste a photo you like in the frame below and read aloud the characters at the bottom.

這相片真的很好看

唸唸看
Read-Aloud

- 做記者的人不可以相信任何人的話。
A person being a reporter cannot believe anyone's statement.

- 不可以只聽片面的話。
Can't just listen to partial statements.

- 更不可以只看相片就自己寫一個故事。
Especially cannot write a story only looking at a photo.

- 一定要小心不能寫錯故事。
Have to be careful to not write any story wrong.

- 這樣才能算是公正的記者。
Then this (person) can count as a just reporter.

恭喜你完成了這一課,請回到第一頁將本課的花朵塗上顏色。
Congratulations! You have completed a lesson. Please color the flower for this lesson on page 1.

14

第四課

Lesson 4 Míng – name; place (e.g. among winners); famous; classifier for people

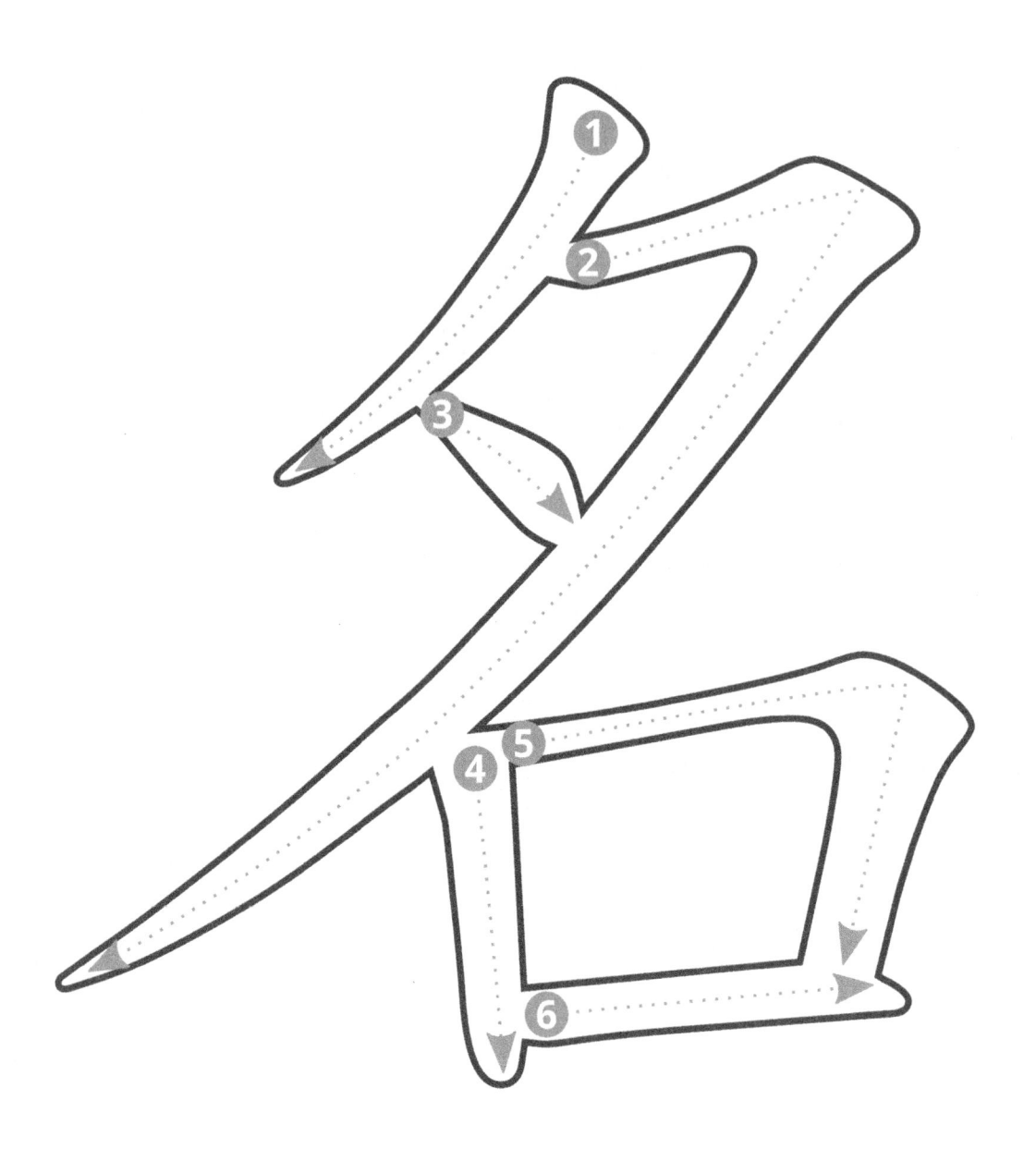

本書中的國字筆順是依據中華民國教育部「常用國字標準字體筆順學習網」的筆劃順序彙編。
The stroke orders of the characters in this workbook follow the stroke orders provided on the "Learning Program for Stroke Order of Frequently Used Chinese Characters" website of the Ministry of Education, R.O.C. (Taiwan).

連連看
Connect the phrases to the correct pictures.

名片 ●

相片 ●

明信片 ●

閱讀測驗。請在正確答案的前面打勾。
Read the following paragraph and answer the questions below.

我的名字叫小明。我有一個哥哥和一個妹妹。哥哥的名字叫大明。妹妹的名字是小美。

1. 小明是家中第幾個小孩？
   ( ) 第一個
   ( ) 第二個
   ( ) 第三個
2. 誰是家裡最小的小孩？
   ( ) 大明
   ( ) 小明
   ( ) 小美

唸唸看
Read-Aloud

- 表姐是一名記者。
  (My) elder female cousin is a reporter.

- 在她的名片上有記者兩個字。
  On her business card, there are the two characters "reporter" on it.

- 她時常會跑去不同的地方工作。
  She often goes to different places to work.

- 工作時還會穿著美麗的衣服。
  When (she) is working, (she) wears beautiful outfits.

- 我相信我也可以當一名好記者。
  I believe I can be a good reporter too.

恭喜你完成了這一課，請回到第一頁將本課的花朵塗上顏色。
Congratulations! You have completed a lesson. Please color the flower for this lesson on page 1.

第五課

Lesson 5 Zhī – possessive particle, literary equivalent of 的

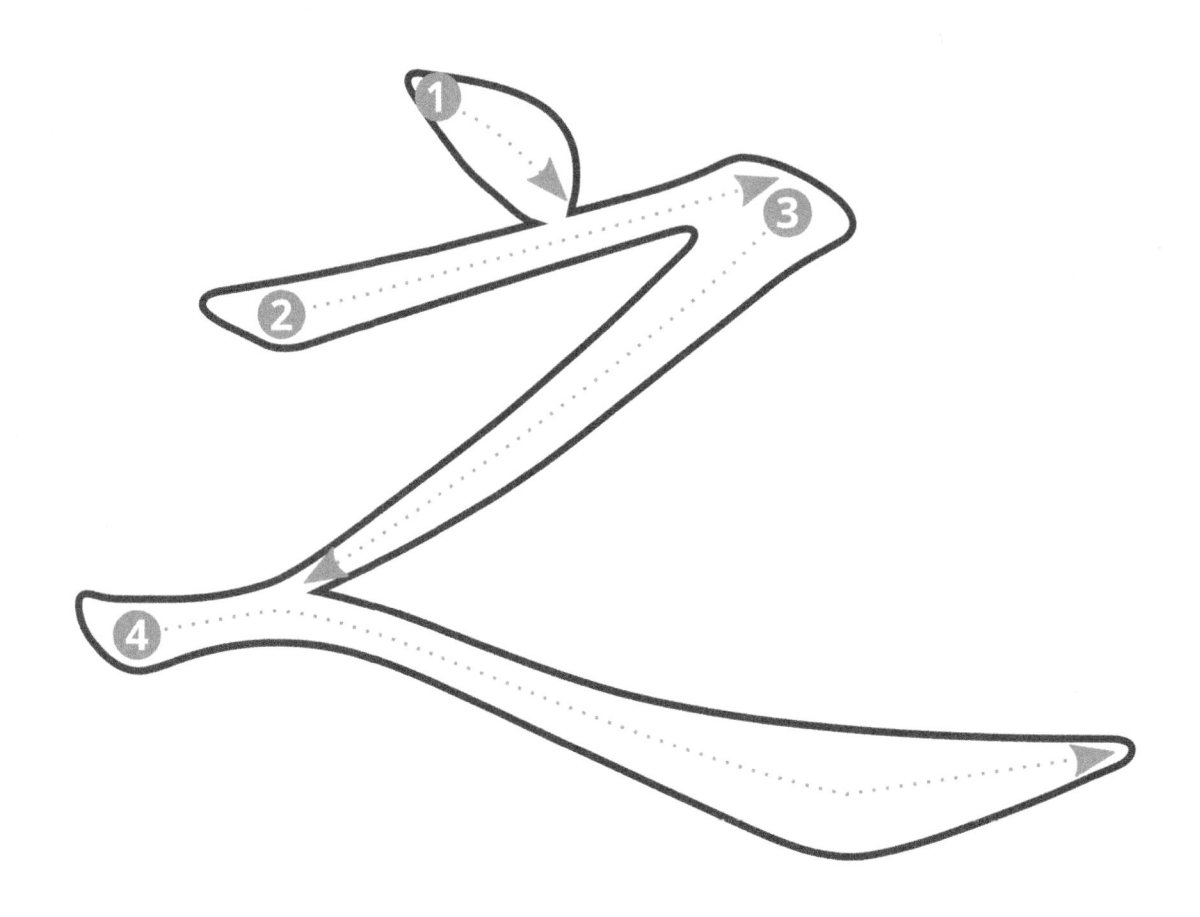

本書中的國字筆順是依據中華民國教育部「常用國字標準字體筆順學習網」的筆劃順序彙編。
The stroke orders of the characters in this workbook follow the stroke orders provided on the "Learning Program for Stroke Order of Frequently Used Chinese Characters" website of the Ministry of Education, R.O.C. (Taiwan).

找出到達「之」字的路。
Find the path leading to the character 之.

之　乏　芝　泛

將「之」字塗色，幫小羊找到草地。
Color the characters 之 to find the path to the field.

唸唸看
Read-Aloud

- 老師問小朋友們長大之後想要當什麼。
  The teacher asked all the kids what they want to be when they grow up.

- 小明想要當銀行家因為他很愛數錢。
  Ming wants to be a banker because he loves to count money.

- 小美想要當電影明星因為她愛看影片。
  Mei wants to be a movie star because she loves to watch films.

- 我長大之後想要當一名記者因為我想上電視。
  When I grow up, I want to be a reporter because I want to be on T.V.

- 相信大家都可以夢想成真。
  (I) believe everyone's dream can become reality.

恭喜你完成了這一課，請回到第一頁將本課的花朵塗上顏色。
Congratulations! You have completed a lesson. Please color the flower for this lesson on page 1.

第六課

Lesson 6 Yè – industry; occupation; employment; school studies

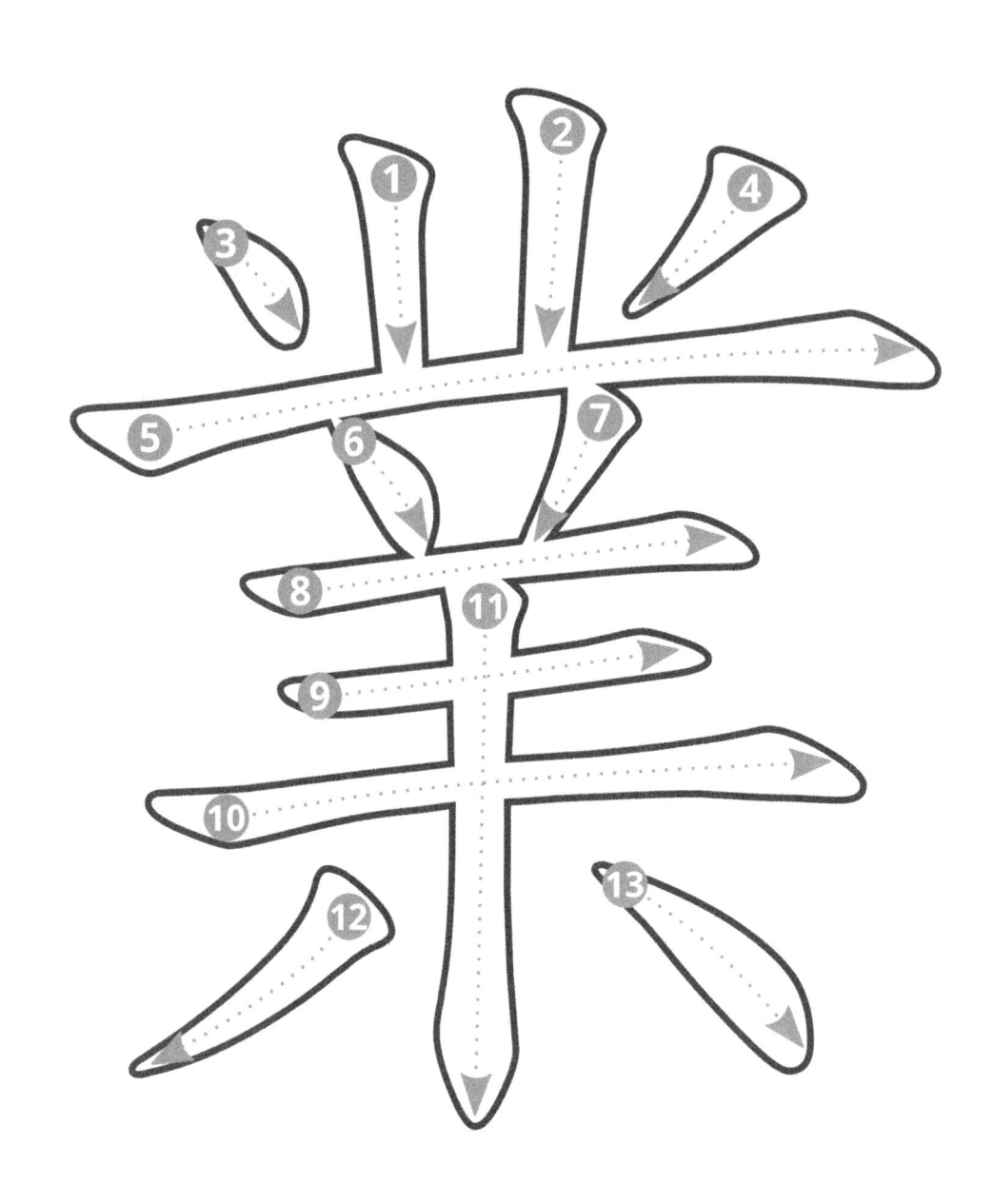

本書中的國字筆順是依據中華民國教育部「常用國字標準字體筆順學習網」的筆劃順序彙編。
The stroke orders of the characters in this workbook follow the stroke orders provided on the "Learning Program for Stroke Order of Frequently Used Chinese Characters" website of the Ministry of Education, R.O.C. (Taiwan).

請圈出對的文字造出正確的語詞。
Please circle the correct characters to form phrases.

工 | 二	打 | 事
業	業

作 | 怎	比 | 行
業	業

24

跟著「業」字從 ➡ 到 ★ 走出迷宮。
Follow the characters 業 from the arrow to the star to exit the maze.

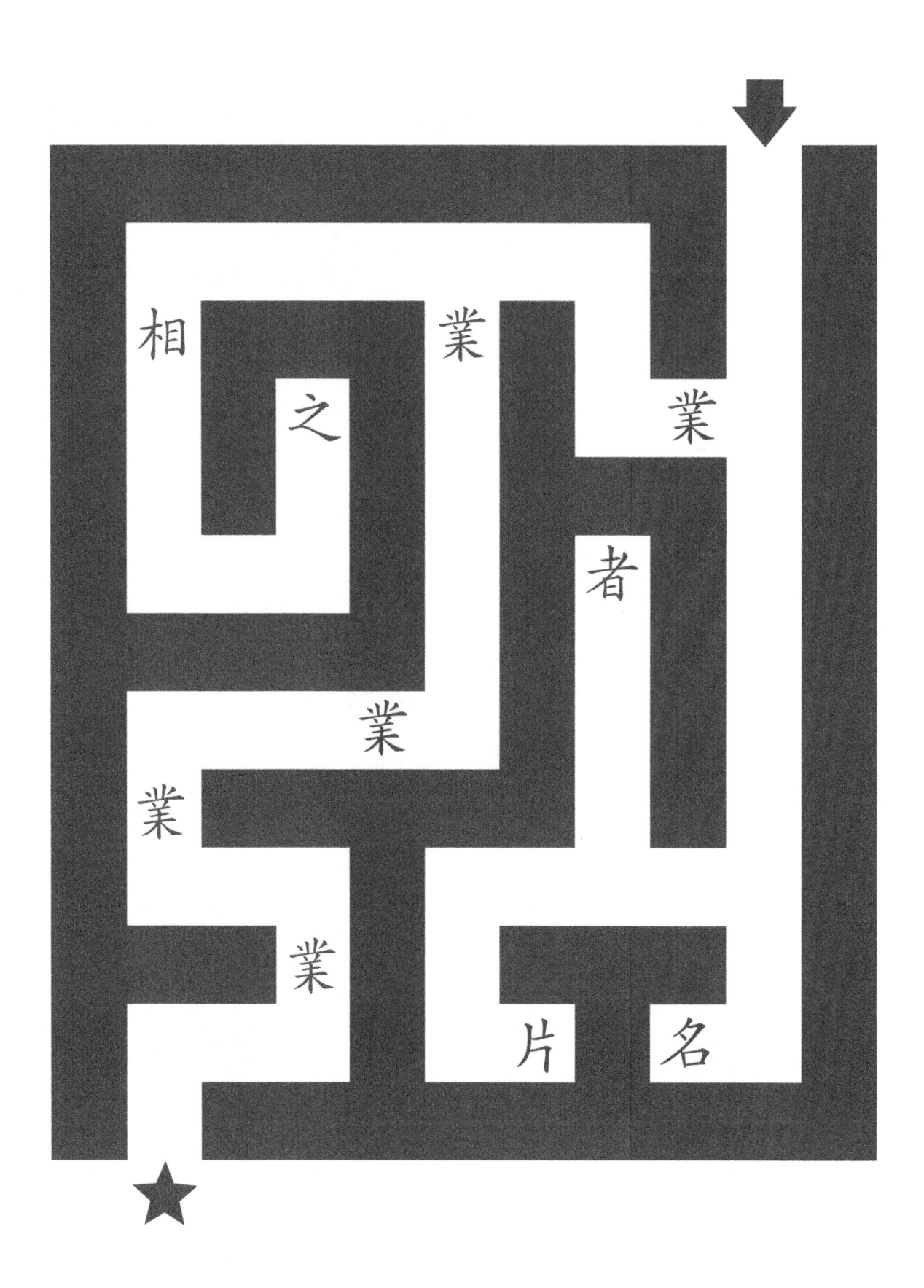

唸唸看
Read-Aloud

- 今天的作業要我們回去問弟弟妹妹長大之後想要做什麼。

  Today's assignment wants us to go home and ask what our little brothers and sisters want to be when they grow up.

- 弟弟想要當美食家因為可以吃好多點心。

  (My) younger brother wants to be a connoisseur because (he) can eat lots of dessert.

- 妹妹想要當一名記者因為她只會學我。

  (My) younger sister wants to be a reporter because she only knows to copy me.

- 哥哥想要當音樂老師並且給我看他做的歌唱教學影片。

  (My) elder brother wants to be a music teacher, and (he) shows me the singing instruction video he made.

- 我覺得這個作業非常有意思。

  I think this assignment is really interesting.

恭喜你完成了這一課，請回到第一頁將本課的花朵塗上顏色。
Congratulations! You have completed a lesson. Please color the flower for this lesson on page 1.

26

第七課

Lesson 7 Tā – it

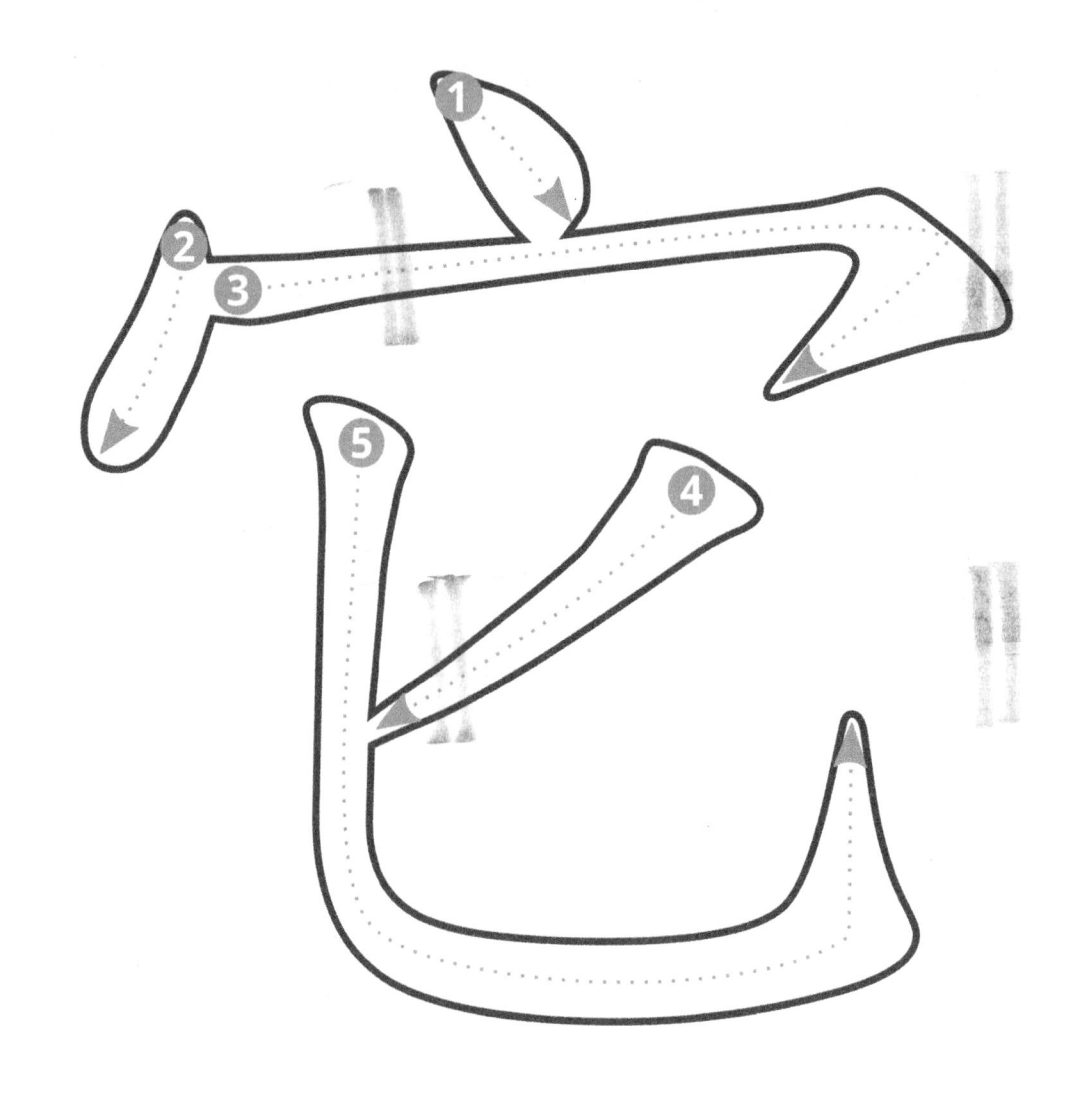

本書中的國字筆順是依據中華民國教育部「常用國字標準字體筆順學習網」的筆劃順序彙編。
The stroke orders of the characters in this workbook follow the stroke orders provided on the "Learning Program for Stroke Order of Frequently Used Chinese Characters" website of the Ministry of Education, R.O.C. (Taiwan).

找出「它」字圈出來。
Find the characters 它 and circle them.

它　　　　　　　七

　　　　　　　　　　　它
北　　　己

　　　　　　　　　化
它　　　它

　　　　　　　花
匕

28

連連看
Connect the characters to the correct pictures.

他 •

• (girl)

她 •

• (teddy bear)

它 •

• (boy)

連連看
Connect the characters to the correct pictures.

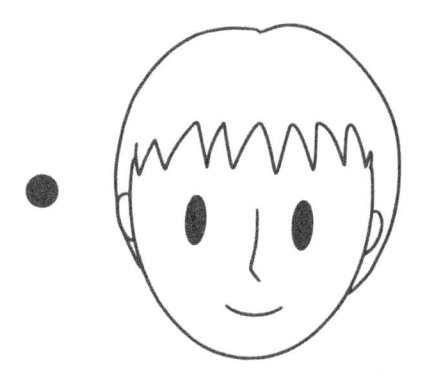

唸唸看
Read-Aloud

- 那個公園之所以有名是因為它裡面有一大片草地。
The reason why that park is famous is because it has a big meadow inside.

- 老師出了一個作業要我們到公園裡寫生。
The teacher's assignment wants us to go to the park to sketch.

- 我的畫裡有綠色的草地、藍色的天空和黃色的花朵。
In my drawing there are green grass, blue sky, and yellow flowers.

- 我還在畫裡畫了三隻小白兔和一條河。
I also drew three little white rabbits and a river in my drawing.

- 老師越看我的畫越滿意，問我可不可以把它送給老師。
The more the teacher looks at my drawing, the more (the teacher) is satisfied. (The teacher) asked me if I could give it to the teacher.

恭喜你完成了這一課，請回到第一頁將本課的花朵塗上顏色。
Congratulations! You have completed a lesson. Please color the flower for this lesson on page 1.

第八課

Lesson 8 Mài – to sell

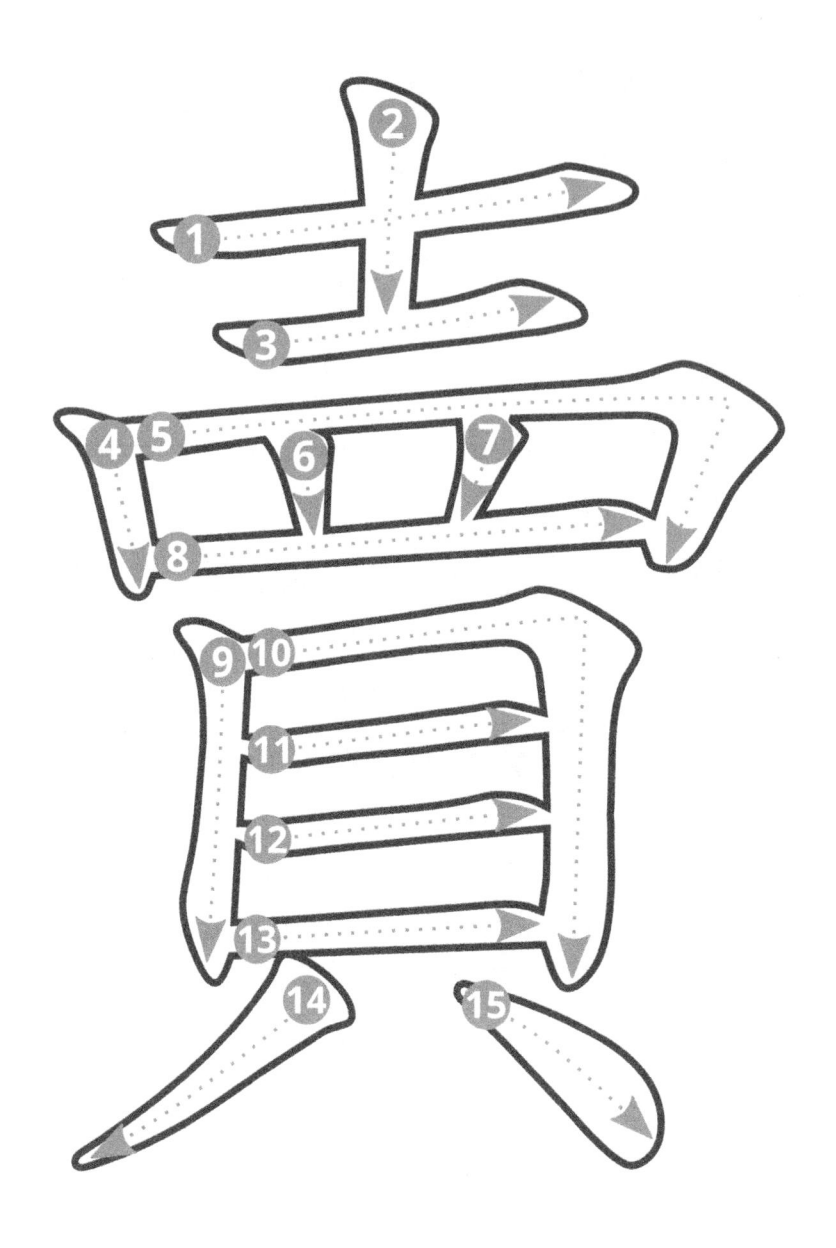

本書中的國字筆順是依據中華民國教育部「常用國字標準字體筆順學習網」的筆劃順序彙編。
The stroke orders of the characters in this workbook follow the stroke orders provided on the "Learning Program for Stroke Order of Frequently Used Chinese Characters" website of the Ministry of Education, R.O.C. (Taiwan).

連連看
Connect the phrases to the correct stores.

賣書 ●　　　　● 玩具店

賣水果 ●　　　● 書店

賣玩具 ●　　　● 水果店

32

圈出可以組成下面文字的部分。
Circle the parts that form the character at the bottom.

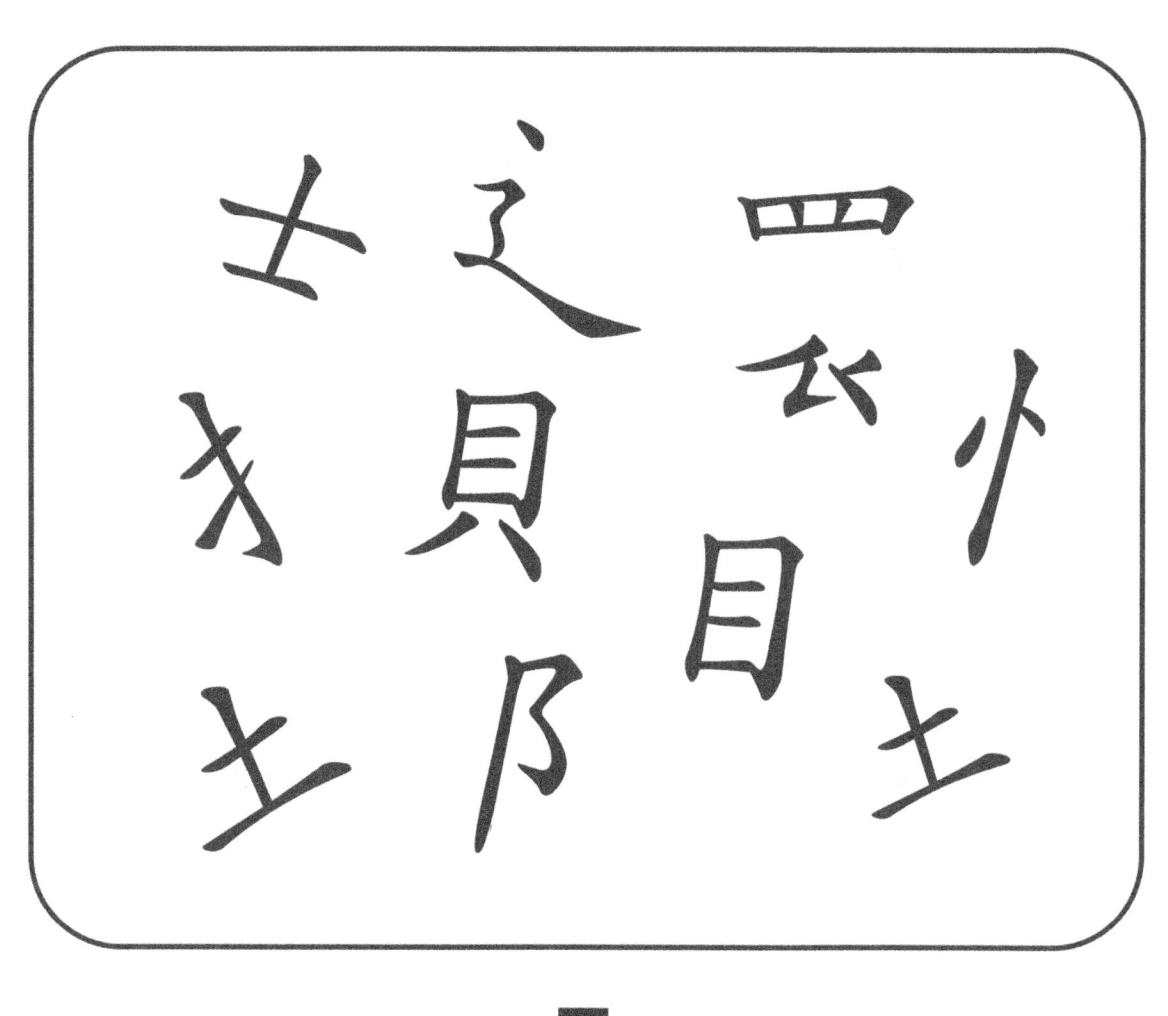

士　辶　　　四　
　　貝　　士　卜
扌　　　　　目
土　阝　　　　土

↓

賣

唸唸看
Read-Aloud

- 我家對面有一間很有名的賣場。
  There is a very famous market across from my house.

- 它裡面有賣好多種東西。
  It sells many different kinds of items inside.

- 我們在裡面買了雞塊吃。
  We bought some chicken nuggets inside to eat.

- 吃完飯之後我們還在裡面的書店買作業本。
  After eating, we also bought workbooks at the bookstore inside.

- 店裡面還有賣玩具和手提包。
  The store also sells toys and handbags.

恭喜你完成了這一課,請回到第一頁將本課的花朵塗上顏色。
Congratulations! You have completed a lesson. Please color the flower for this lesson on page 1.

第九課

Lesson 9 Xǔ – to allow; somewhat; perhaps

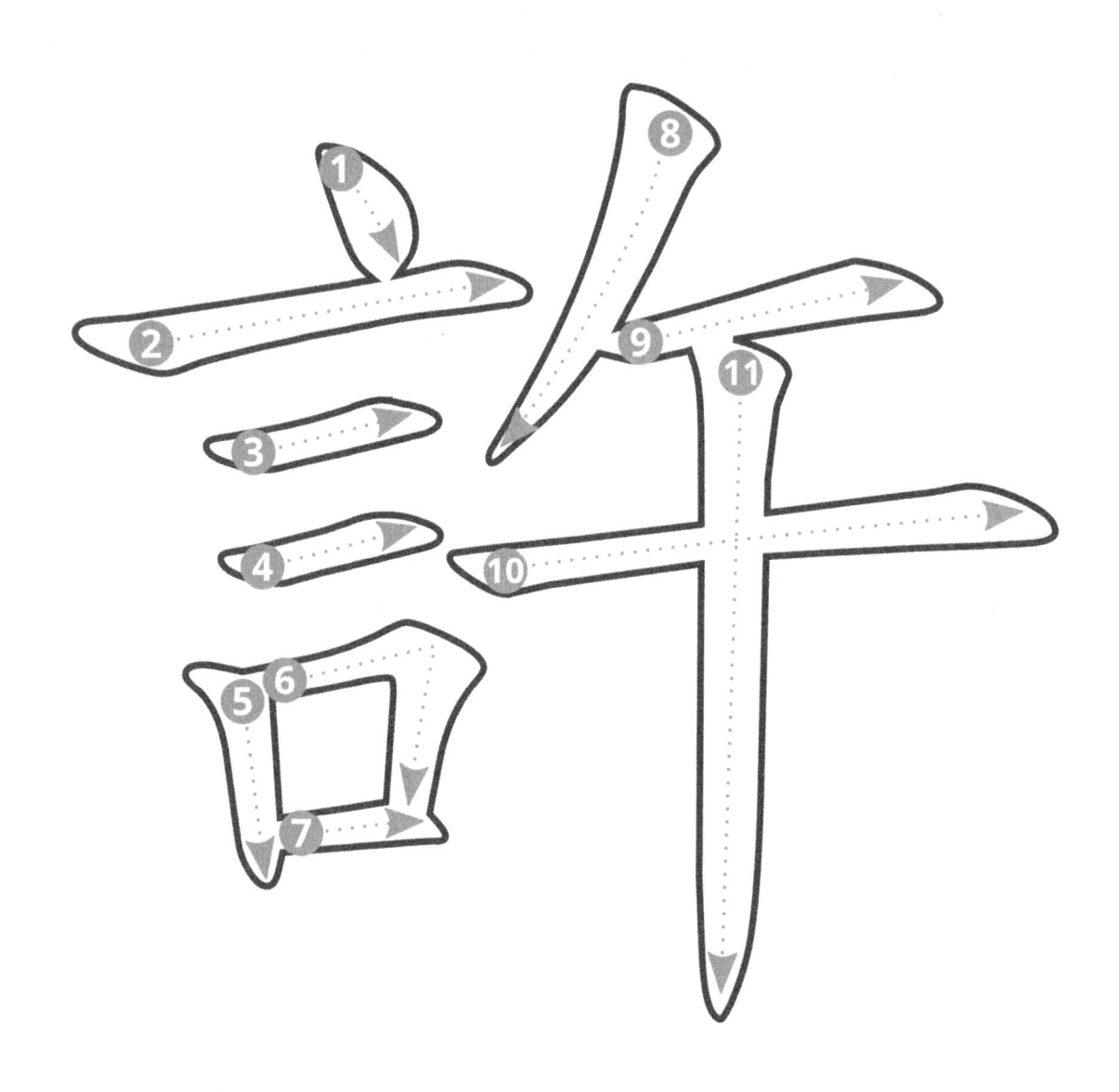

本書中的國字筆順是依據中華民國教育部「常用國字標準字體筆順學習網」的筆劃順序彙編。
The stroke orders of the characters in this workbook follow the stroke orders provided on the "Learning Program for Stroke Order of Frequently Used Chinese Characters" website of the Ministry of Education, R.O.C. (Taiwan).

將左邊的語詞連到右邊的詞意。
Connect the phrases in the boxes on the left to the correct definitions in the boxes on the right.

作者 •	• 一點點
少許 •	• 寫書的人
作業 •	• 回家功課

36

請將下方的字格剪下來讓孩子選擇正確的字貼上。
Please cut out the characters at the bottom and paste the correct one.

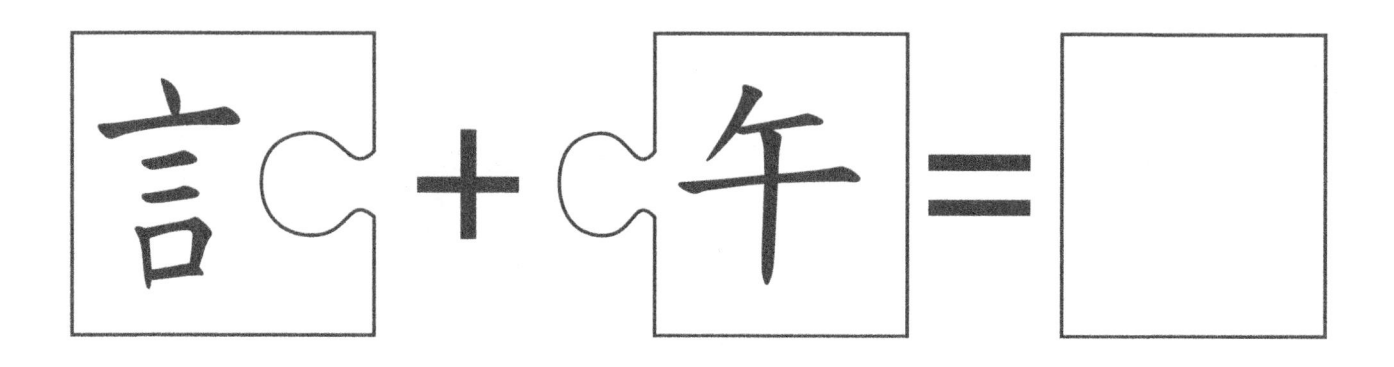

言 + 午 = 　

| 言 | 午 | 許 | 話 | 說 |

唸唸看
Read-Aloud

- 這次的作業我寫了一個故事。
  I wrote a story for (my) assignment this time.

- 外太空之中有一顆紅色的星球住著許多怪物。
  There is a red planet with many monsters in outer space.

- 星球上有賣許多可怕又發黑的食物。
  On the planet (they) sell many scary and black food.

- 你要是吃了它們就會倒在地上再也起不來了。
  If you eat them, (you) will fall to the floor and never get up again.

- 如果你到了那顆星球上,請不要吃那裡的食物。
  If you arrive at that planet, please do not eat the food there.

恭喜你完成了這一課,請回到第一頁將本課的花朵塗上顏色。
Congratulations! You have completed a lesson. Please color the flower for this lesson on page 1.

第十課

Lesson 10 Mù – eye; goal

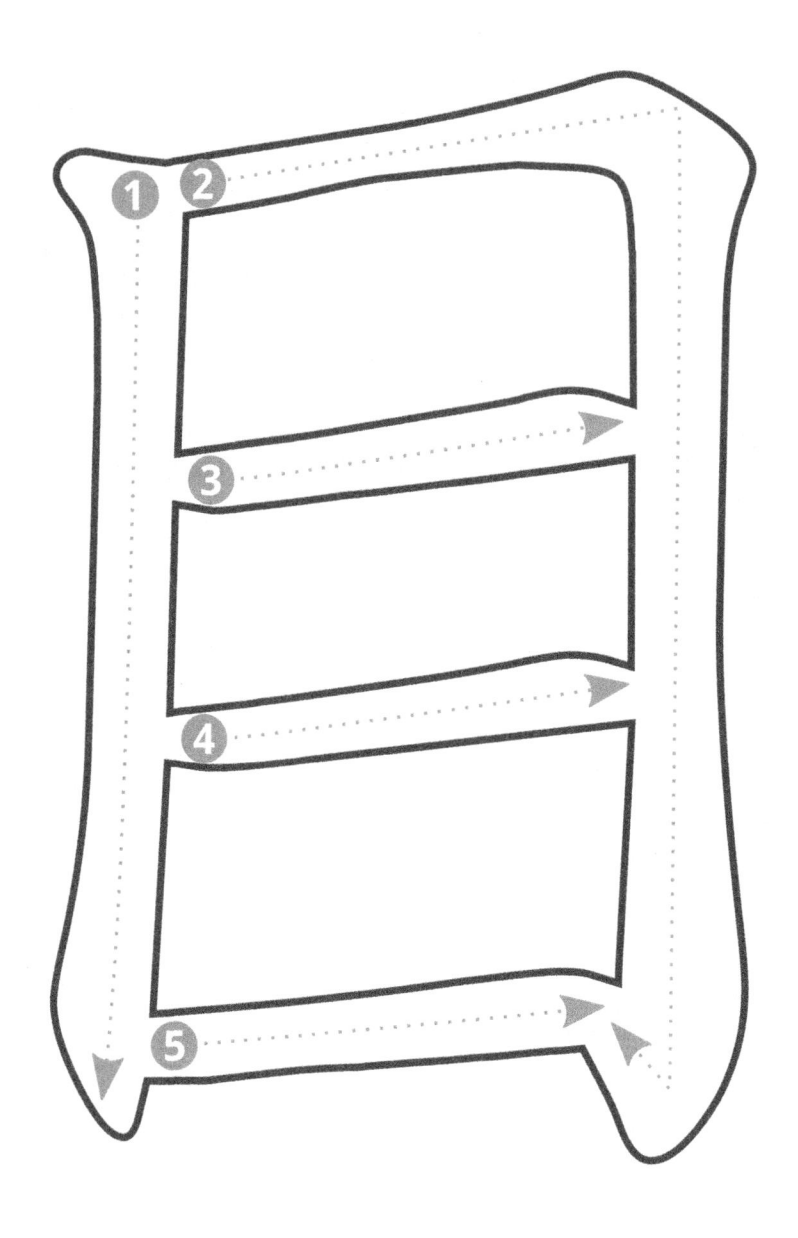

本書中的國字筆順是依據中華民國教育部「常用國字標準字體筆順學習網」的筆劃順序彙編。
The stroke orders of the characters in this workbook follow the stroke orders provided on the "Learning Program for Stroke Order of Frequently Used Chinese Characters" website of the Ministry of Education, R.O.C. (Taiwan).

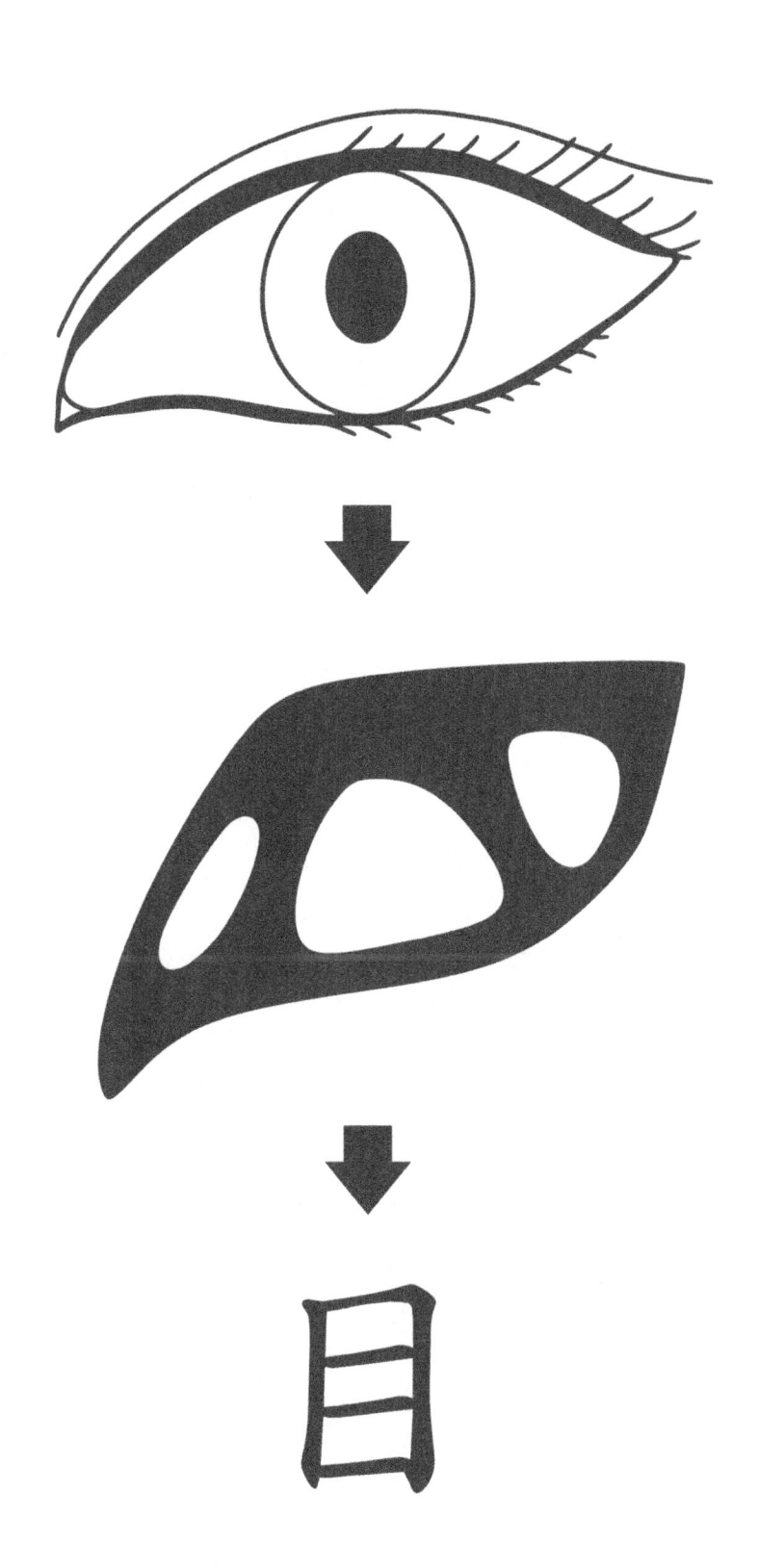

「目」是象形字，它看起來就像人的一隻眼睛。
The character 目 is a pictograph. It looks like an eye.

「目」是象形字，它看起來就像人的一隻眼睛。
The character 目 is a pictograph. It looks like an eye.

閱讀測驗。請在正確答案的前面打勾。
Read the following paragraph and answer the questions below.

我們正在電視機前看一場足球賽。目前比賽進行到了下半場，分數是三比二。紅隊拿了三分，藍隊二分。比賽最終會怎樣，目前還不知道。

1. 我們在哪看球賽？
　（　）現場
　（　）電視機前
　（　）沒有看球賽
2. 比賽目前進行到哪了？
　（　）上半場
　（　）下半場
　（　）不知道

唸唸看
Read-Aloud

- 上次作業的故事還沒有寫完，所以我這次要把它寫完。
  (I) haven't finished the story assignment from last time, therefore I am finishing it this time.

- 在賣許多可怕食物的星球上還有一個怪物的頭目。
  On the planet that sells many scary foods also has a monster leader.

- 頭目的力氣很大，可以把一顆球打飛到太空。
  The leader has great strength and can hit a ball into space.

- 有一天頭目吃了發黑的食物。
  One day the leader ate food that is black.

- 之後就躺在床上睡到今天都還沒有起來。
  Then, (the leader) lay on a bed to sleep and hasn't woken up today yet.

恭喜你完成了這一課，請回到第一頁將本課的花朵塗上顏色。
Congratulations! You have completed a lesson. Please color the flower for this lesson on page 1.

第十一課

Lesson 11 Tí – topic; question

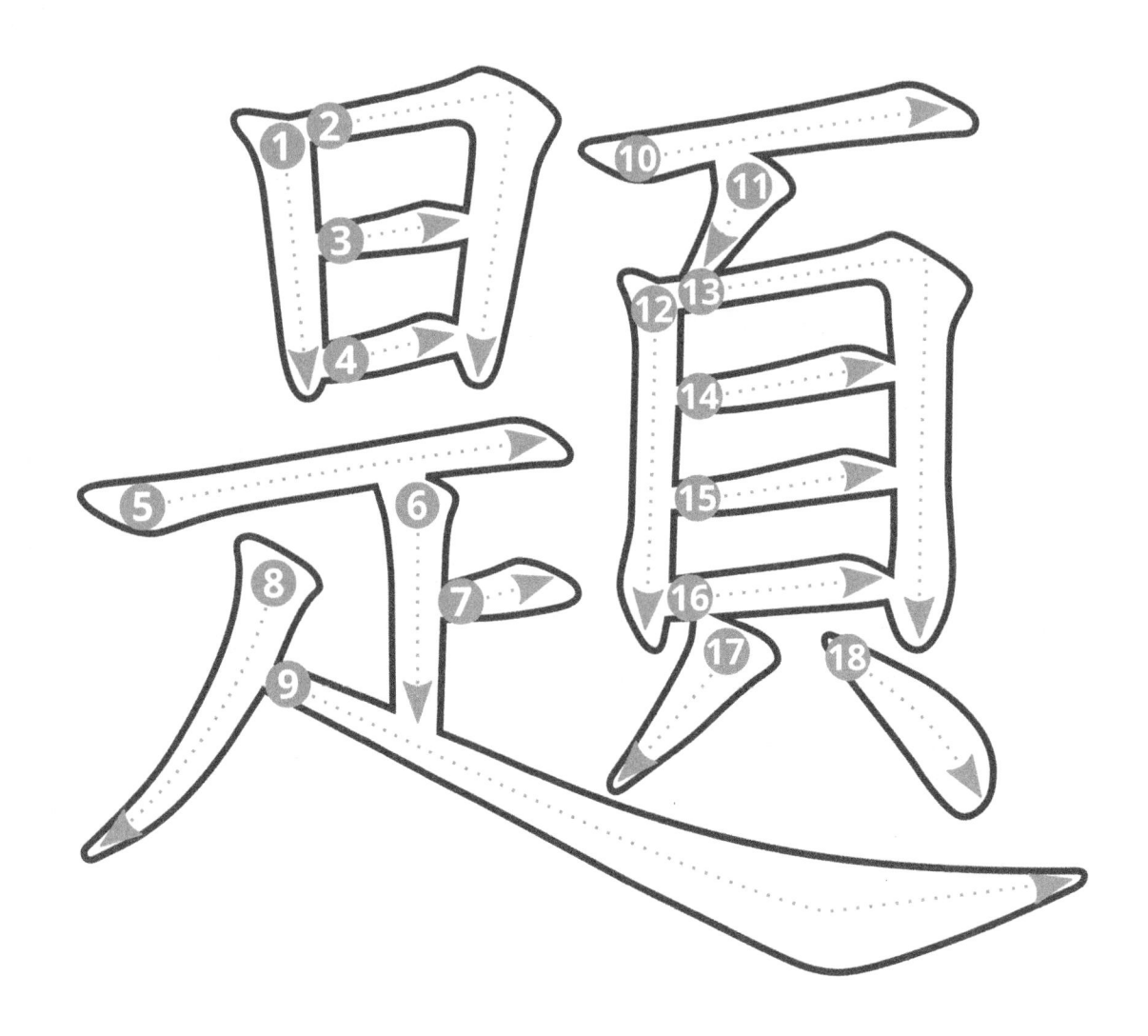

本書中的國字筆順是依據中華民國教育部「常用國字標準字體筆順學習網」的筆劃順序彙編。
The stroke orders of the characters in this workbook follow the stroke orders provided on the "Learning Program for Stroke Order of Frequently Used Chinese Characters" website of the Ministry of Education, R.O.C. (Taiwan).

請將有「題」字的區塊著色。
Please color the areas with the character 題.

44

連連看一樣的字。
Match the charaters.

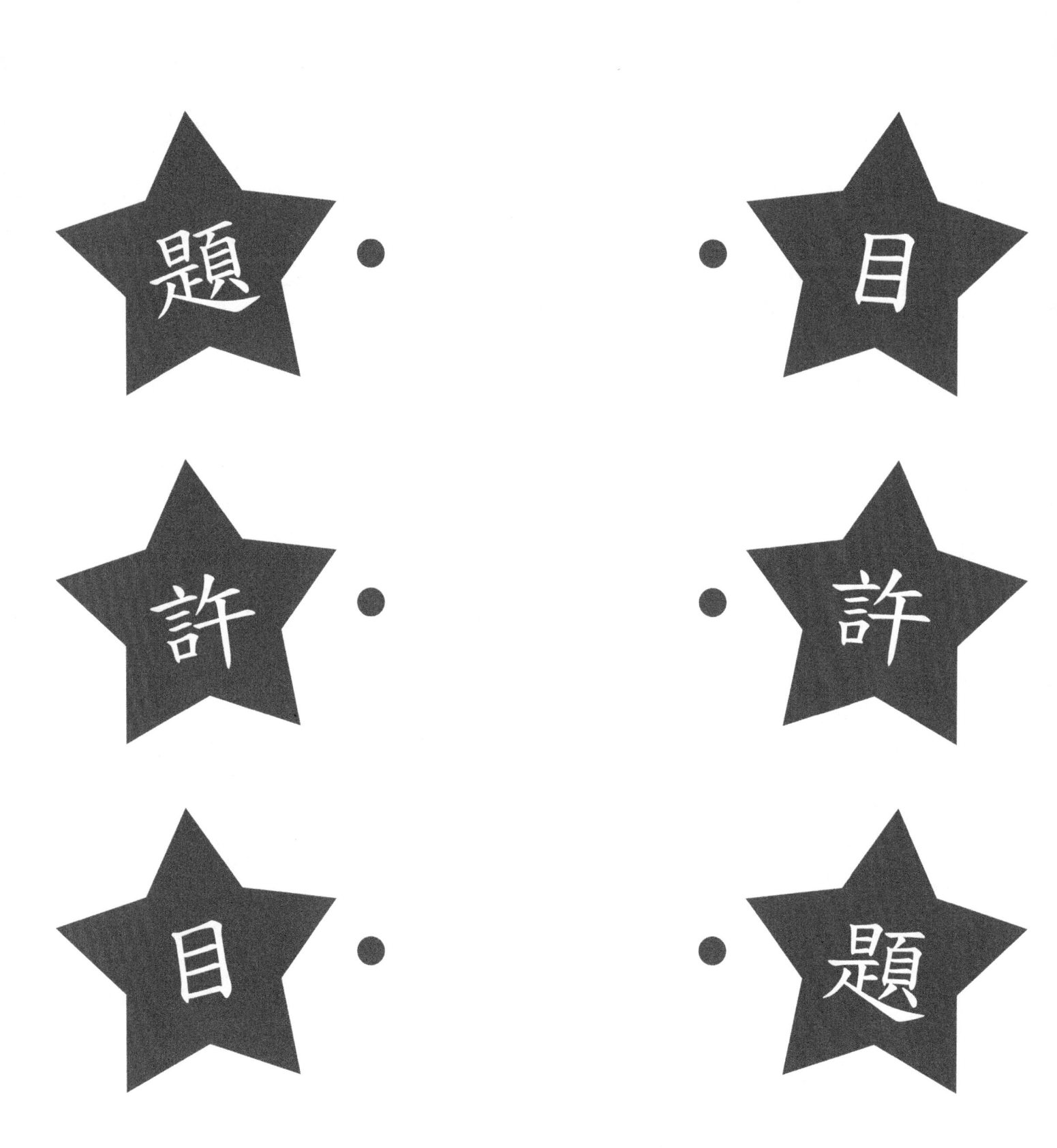

題　　　目

許　　　許

目　　　題

唸唸看
Read-Aloud

- 我問你幾道數學題目，看看你知不知道怎麼算吧？
  (Let) me ask you some math questions and see if you know how to calculate.

- 小女孩在賣魚，她本來有七條，客人買光了所有的魚。
  A little girl is selling fish. She originally has seven fish, and the customer buys all the fish.

- 請問她還有幾條魚？
  How many fish does she still have?

- 王先生在賣毛衣，現在是六月所以賣了許多天以後都沒有人買它們。
  Mr. Wong is selling sweaters. It is June now, therefore after selling (them) for several days, no one buys them.

- 題目是請問王先生一共賣了幾件毛衣？
  The question is: How many sweaters did Mr. Wong sell?

恭喜你完成了這一課，請回到第一頁將本課的花朵塗上顏色。
Congratulations! You have completed a lesson. Please color the flower for this lesson on page 1.

第十二課

Lesson 12 Ne – particle indicating that a previously asked question is to be applied to the preceding word ("What about ...?", "And ...?"); particle indicating strong affirmation

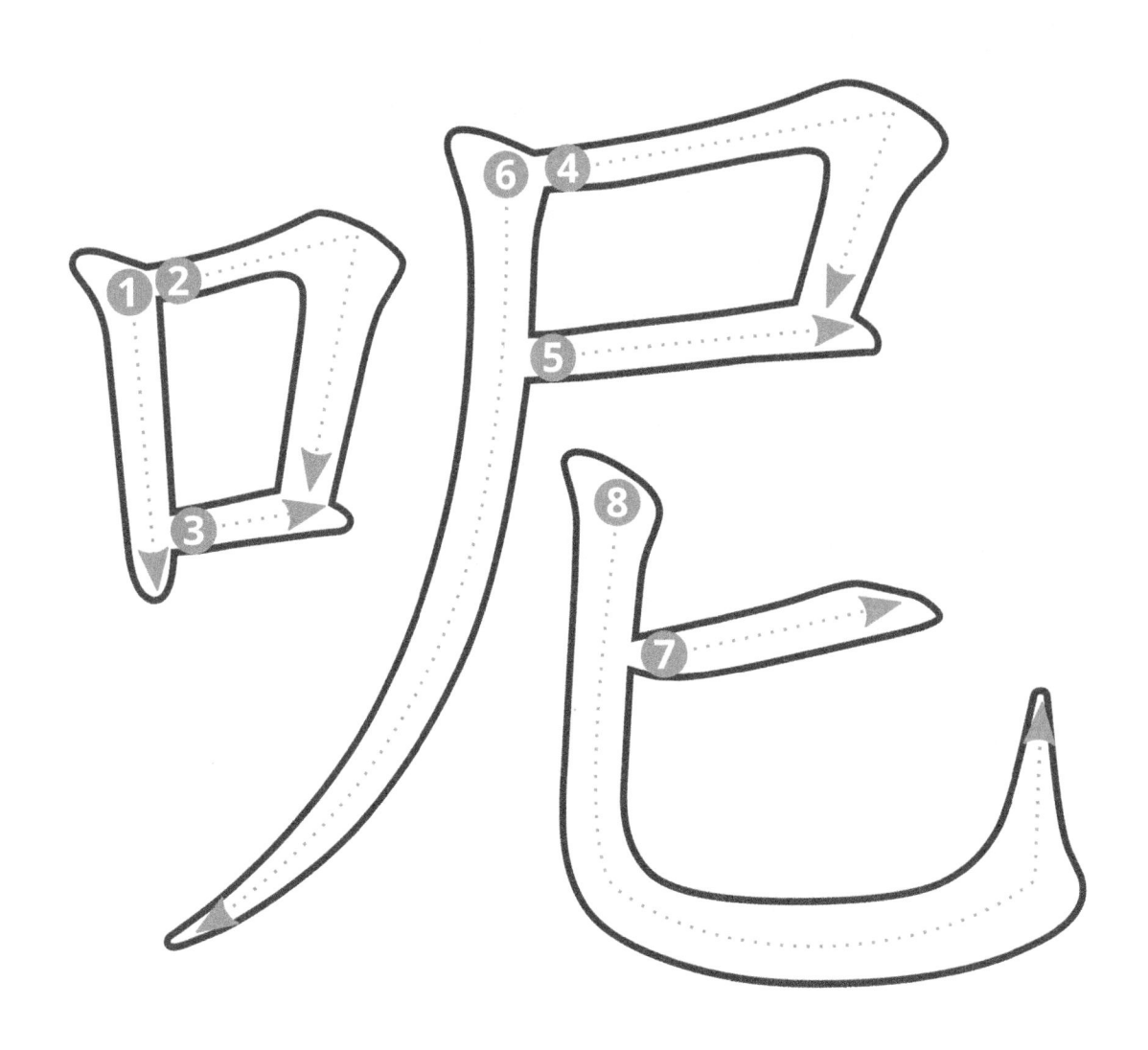

本書中的國字筆順是依據中華民國教育部「常用國字標準字體筆順學習網」的筆劃順序彙編。
The stroke orders of the characters in this workbook follow the stroke orders provided on the "Learning Program for Stroke Order of Frequently Used Chinese Characters" website of the Ministry of Education, R.O.C. (Taiwan).

請將三個相同的字連成一線。
Please connect the same characters to win the tic-tac-toe.

47

妮	妮	尼
呢	呢	呢
尼	尼	妮

找出「呢」字圈出來。
Find the characters 呢 and circle them.

呢　呢　妮　尼　呢　呢　吧　戶　七

唸唸看
Read-Aloud

- 數學課本中常常有許多好笑的題目。

  There are often many funny questions in the math textbook.

- 像是院子裡有八隻鳥、十隻羊和五隻山貓，一共有幾隻動物呢？

  Like there are 8 birds, 10 goats, and 5 mountain lions in the yard. How many animals are there in total?

- 我家的院子不是動物園，不可能有足夠的空間放那麼多動物。

  My yard is not a zoo, it is not possible to have enough space for that many animals.

- 又像是爸爸喝了九杯牛奶後又喝了四杯，他一共喝了幾杯呢？

  Another example is: After Dad drank 9 cups of milk, he drank four more cups. How many cups of milk did he drink in total?

- 賣牛奶的人一定很開心，可是誰會喝那麼多杯的牛奶呢？

  The person selling milk must be very happy. But who will drink that many cups of milk?

恭喜你完成了這一課，請回到第一頁將本課的花朵塗上顏色。

Congratulations! You have completed a lesson. Please color the flower for this lesson on page 1.

第十三課

Lesson 13 Nán – difficult
Nàn – disaster

本書中的國字筆順是依據中華民國教育部「常用國字標準字體筆順學習網」的筆劃順序彙編。
The stroke orders of the characters in this workbook follow the stroke orders provided on the "Learning Program for Stroke Order of Frequently Used Chinese Characters" website of the Ministry of Education, R.O.C. (Taiwan).

閱讀測驗。請在正確答案的前面打勾。
Read the following paragraph and answer the questions below.

小美平常上課很用心，回家都會先把功課做完才出去玩，所以今天老師出的題目一點都難不倒她。

1. 小美回家都先做什麼事情？
   （ ）寫功課
   （ ）出去玩
   （ ）看電視
2. 小美為什麼覺得題目不難？
   （ ）回家不寫功課都在玩
   （ ）上課用心，回家先寫功課
   （ ）老師放水

跟著「難」字從 ➡ 到 ★ 走出迷宮。
Follow the characters 難 from the arrow to the star to exit the maze.

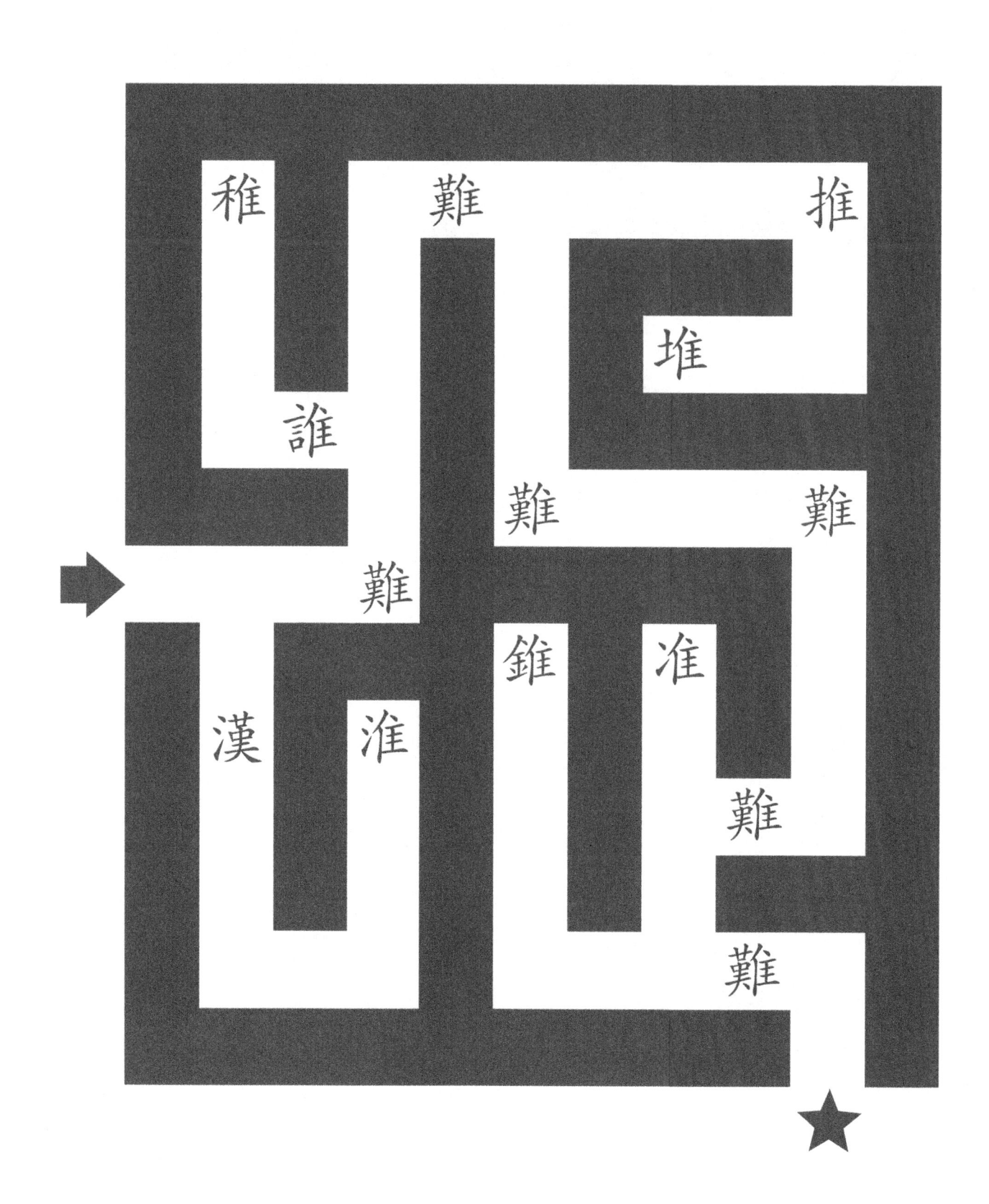

唸唸看
Read-Aloud

- 賽馬場裡的馬兒跑得很快。
  The horses on the racetrack run very fast.

- 賽車場裡的賽車也跑得很快。
  The race cars on the racetrack run very fast too.

- 是賽車跑得比較快，還是馬跑得快，這個問題並不難。
  Is the race car faster or the horses faster? This is not a hard question.

- 但是如果我把題目改成車比馬快多少呢？
  But if I change the question to how much faster is the car than the horses?

- 也許你就會不知道了，因為這個問題比較難。
  Maybe you will not know, because this question is harder.

恭喜你完成了這一課，請回到第一頁將本課的花朵塗上顏色。
Congratulations! You have completed a lesson. Please color the flower for this lesson on page 1.

第十四課
Lesson 14 Yòu – right

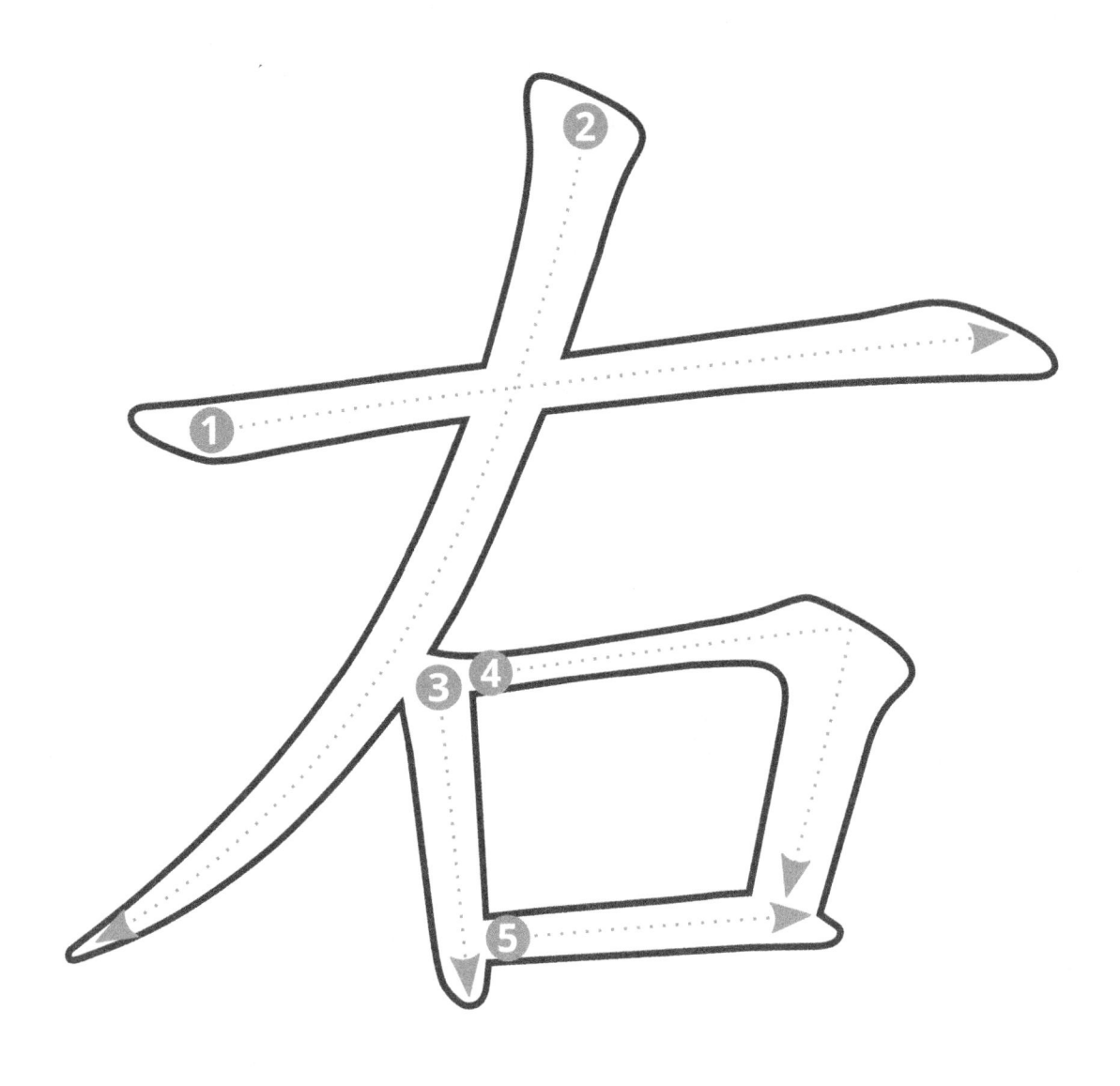

本書中的國字筆順是依據中華民國教育部「常用國字標準字體筆順學習網」的筆劃順序彙編。
The stroke orders of the characters in this workbook follow the stroke orders provided on the "Learning Program for Stroke Order of Frequently Used Chinese Characters" website of the Ministry of Education, R.O.C. (Taiwan).

唸出兩人的對話。
Read the dialog below.

要怎麼走才可以回到家？

往前走兩步然後向右，
再往前走兩步然後再向右，
向右後往前走兩步再向右，
最後往前走兩步就到了。

那不就回到了本來的地方？

因為你本來就在家裡！

56

請將所有向右的箭頭上色並唸出下方的文字。
Please color all the arrows that point to the right and read aloud the characters at the bottom.

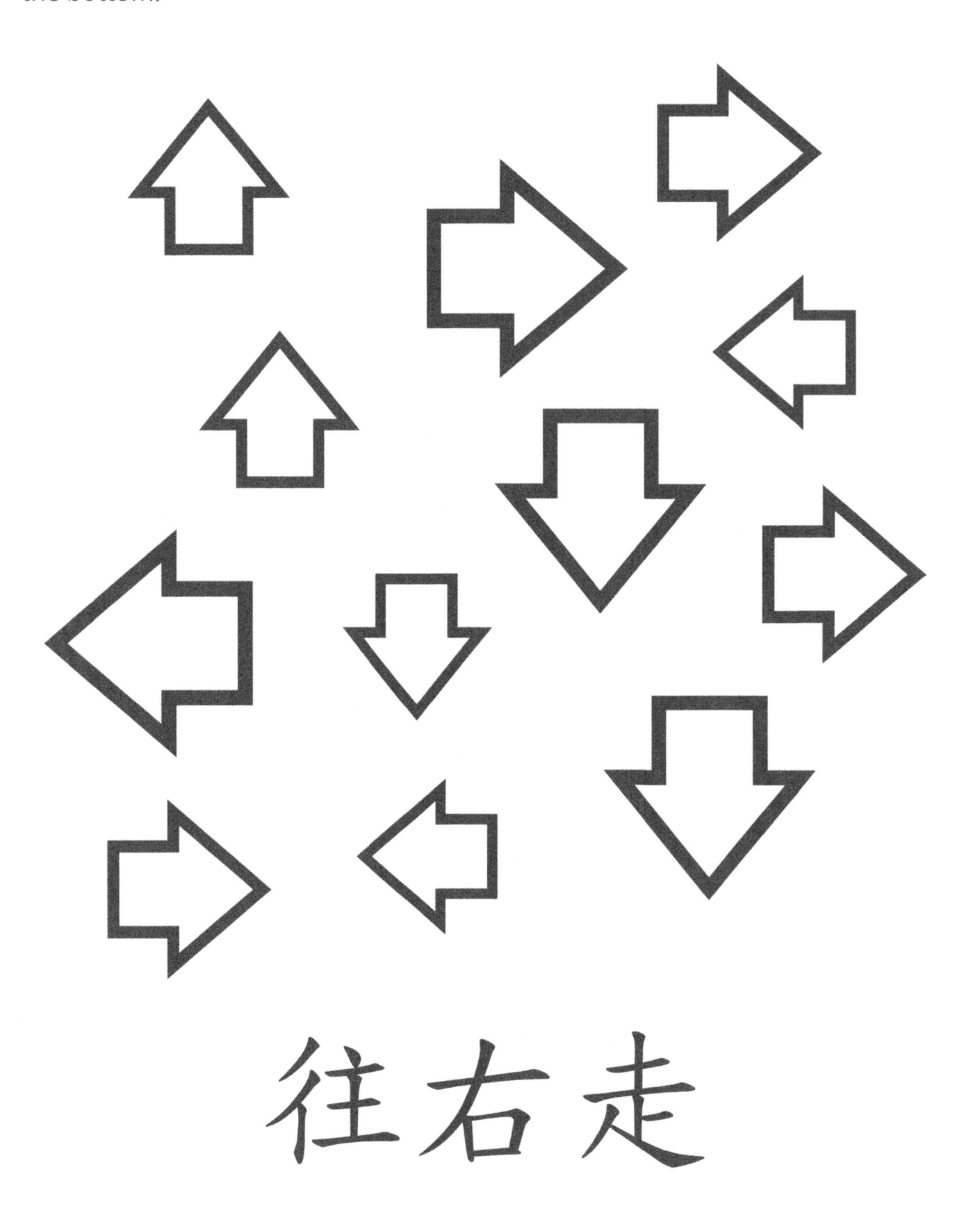

往右走

唸唸看
Read-Aloud

- 早上太陽是從樹的那邊出來的。
  The morning sun rises from the direction of that tree.

- 晚上太陽是在山的右方落下的。
  The sun sets at the right side of the mountain during evening.

- 樹的那邊一定是東邊而山的右邊一定是西邊。
  The side the tree is at must be east and the right side of the mountain must be west.

- 那下雨下個不停的時候要如何找到對的方向呢？
  So when it is raining non stop, how do (we) find the correct direction?

- 這真的是一道很難的題目。
  This is a really difficult question.

恭喜你完成了這一課，請回到第一頁將本課的花朵塗上顏色。
Congratulations! You have completed a lesson. Please color the flower for this lesson on page 1.

第十五課

Lesson 15 Zuǒ – left

本書中的國字筆順是依據中華民國教育部「常用國字標準字體筆順學習網」的筆劃順序彙編。
The stroke orders of the characters in this workbook follow the stroke orders provided on the "Learning Program for Stroke Order of Frequently Used Chinese Characters" website of the Ministry of Education, R.O.C. (Taiwan).

請將下方的圖剪下來讓孩子貼到正確的位置上。
Please cut out the pictures at the bottom and paste them to the correct sides.

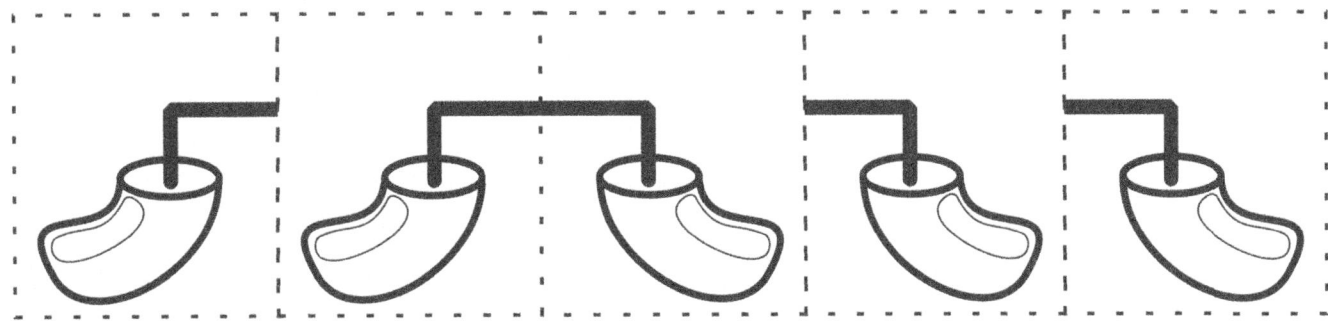

請按照圖中的指示圈出正確的圖案。
Please circle the correct pictures according to the characters in the boxes.

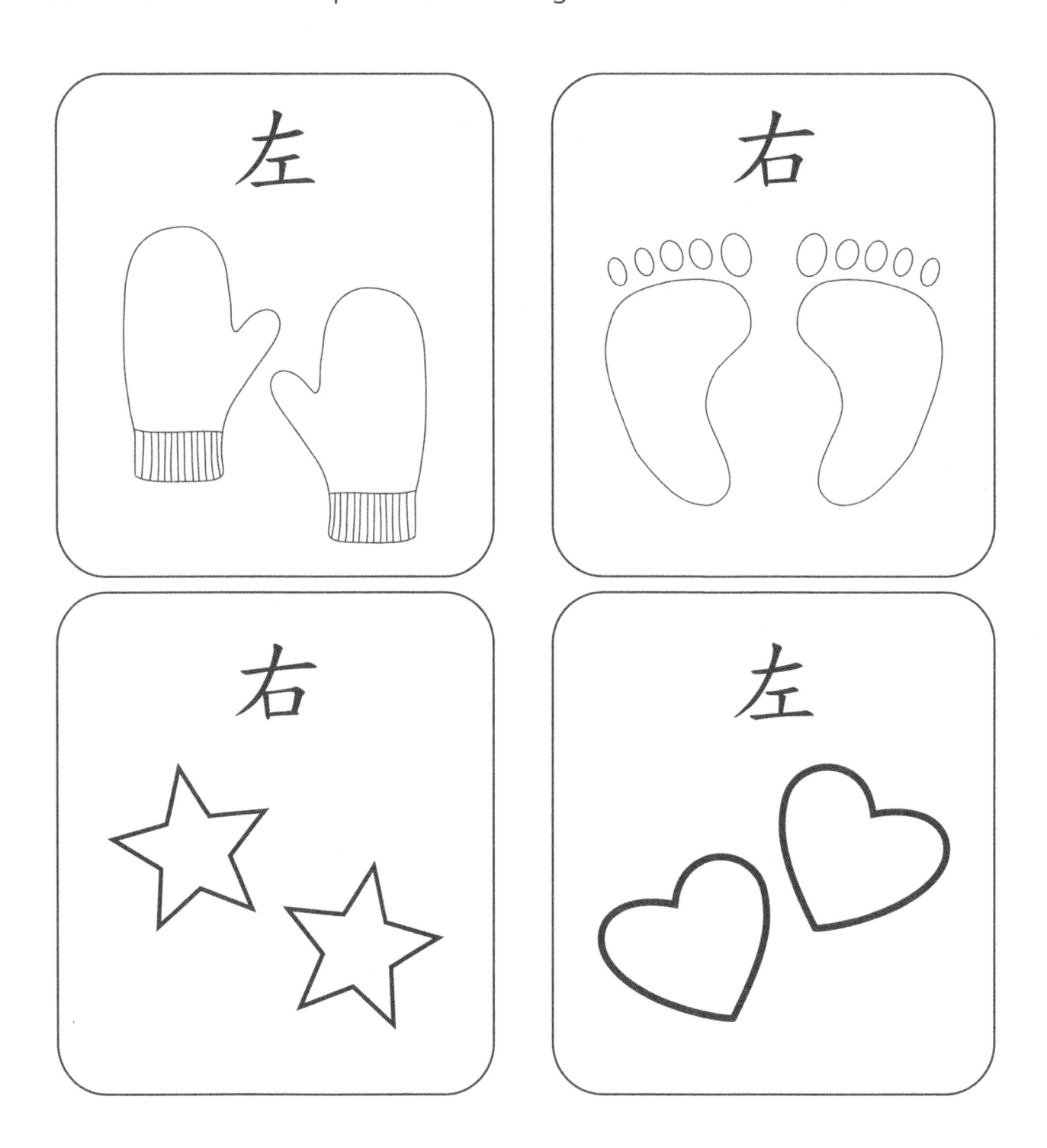

唸唸看
Read-Aloud

- 弟弟的方向感不好，往往左右不分。
  (My) younger brother has a bad sense of direction, (he) often can't tell left from right.

- 有一次我帶弟弟到市場裡買東西。
  I took (my) younger brother to the market to buy things once.

- 弟弟沒有跟好，我往前走時他往左邊走了。
  (My) younger brother didn't follow me. When I walked forward, he walked to the left side.

- 我要在哪找到弟弟變成了一個大難題呢。
  Where can I find (my) younger brother became a huge problem (for me).

- 最終還是找到他了，不過下次我不許弟弟離開我半步。
  At last, I still found him, but next time I am not allowing (my) younger brother to leave my side.

恭喜你完成了這一課，請回到第一頁將本課的花朵塗上顏色。
Congratulations! You have completed a lesson. Please color the flower for this lesson on page 1.

第十六課

Lesson 16 Ān – calm; quiet; safe; to find a place for; to install

本書中的國字筆順是依據中華民國教育部「常用國字標準字體筆順學習網」的筆劃順序彙編。
The stroke orders of the characters in this workbook follow the stroke orders provided on the "Learning Program for Stroke Order of Frequently Used Chinese Characters" website of the Ministry of Education, R.O.C. (Taiwan).

請將有「安」字的安全帽著色。
Please color the helmets with the character 安.

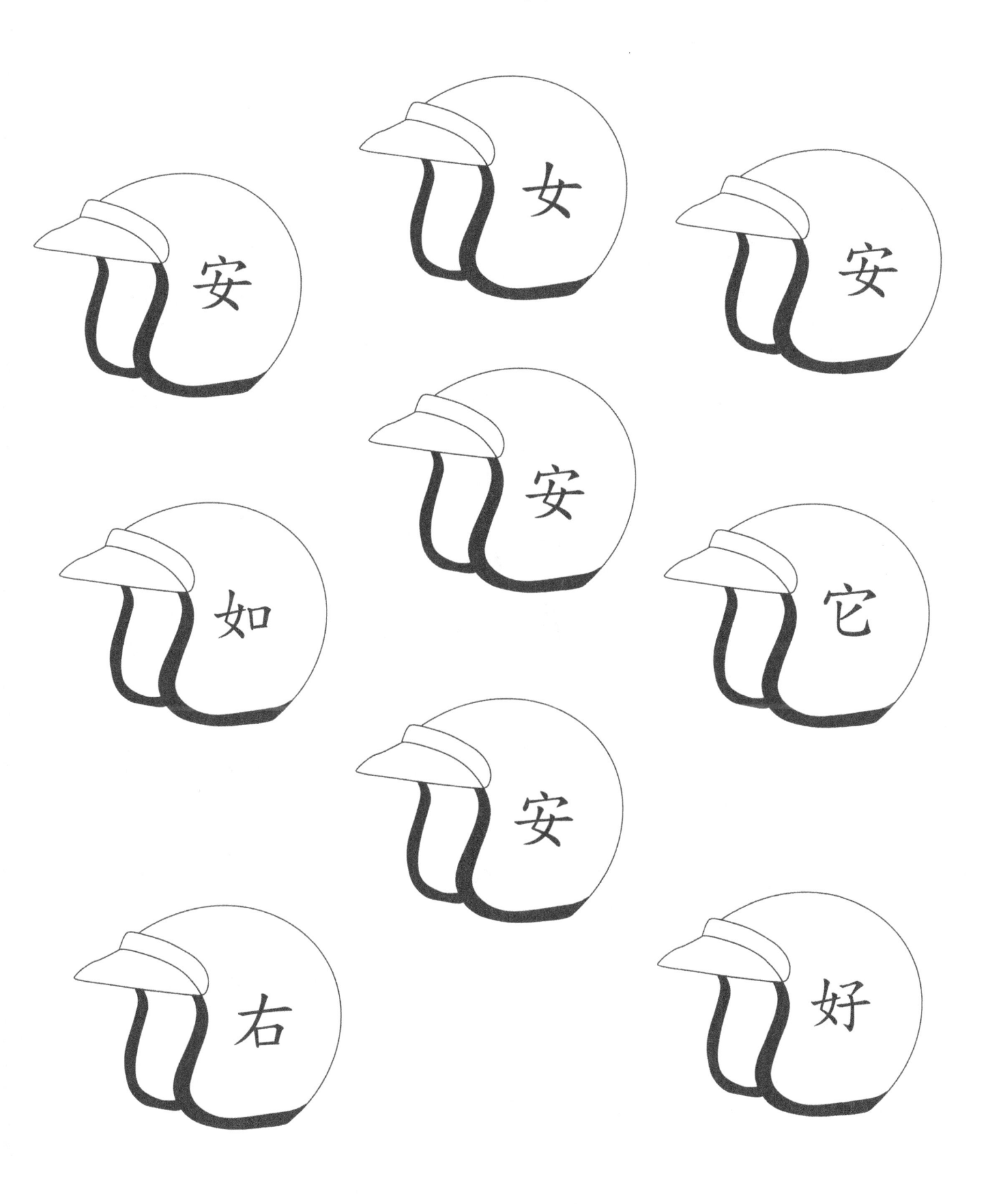

唸出下面的語詞。
Read aloud the phrases in the bubbles.

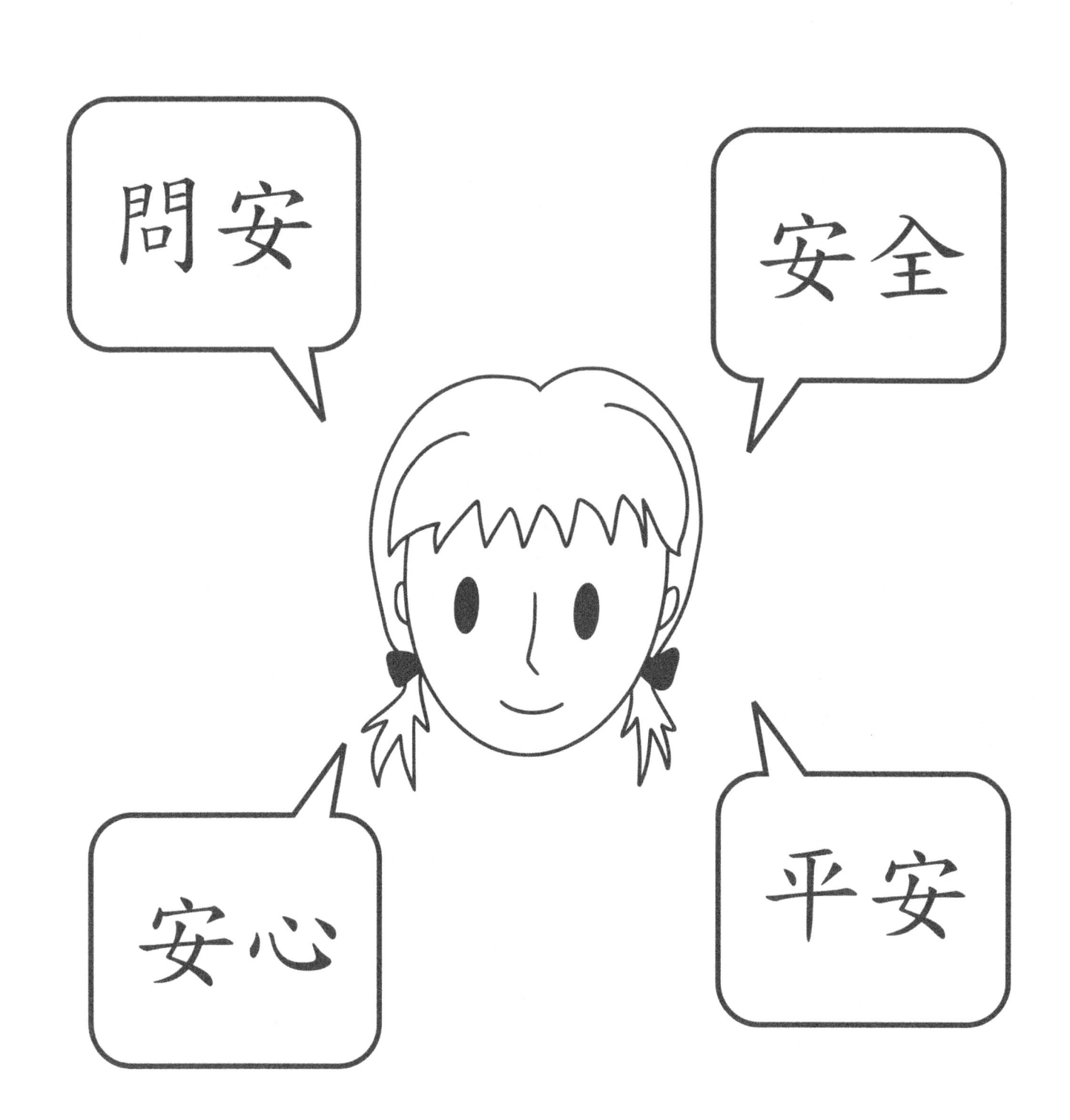

問安

安全

安心

平安

唸唸看
Read-Aloud

- 右邊的那一條路比較安全，但是離目的地比較遠。
The road on the right is safer, but it is farther from the destination.

- 左邊的那一條路比較難走，但是離目的地比較近。
The road on the left is more difficult to take, but it is closer to the destination.

- 你會走哪一條路呢？
Which road will you take?

- 我覺得我會走安全的路。
I think I will take the safer road.

- 理由是我不想要受傷。
The reason is I don't want to be injured.

恭喜你完成了這一課，請回到第一頁將本課的花朵塗上顏色。
Congratulations! You have completed a lesson. Please color the flower for this lesson on page 1.

第十七課

Lesson 17 Qīng – clear; to clean up

本書中的國字筆順是依據中華民國教育部「常用國字標準字體筆順學習網」的筆劃順序彙編。
The stroke orders of the characters in this workbook follow the stroke orders provided on the "Learning Program for Stroke Order of Frequently Used Chinese Characters" website of the Ministry of Education, R.O.C. (Taiwan).

圈出可以組成下面文字的部分。
Circle the parts that form the character at the bottom.

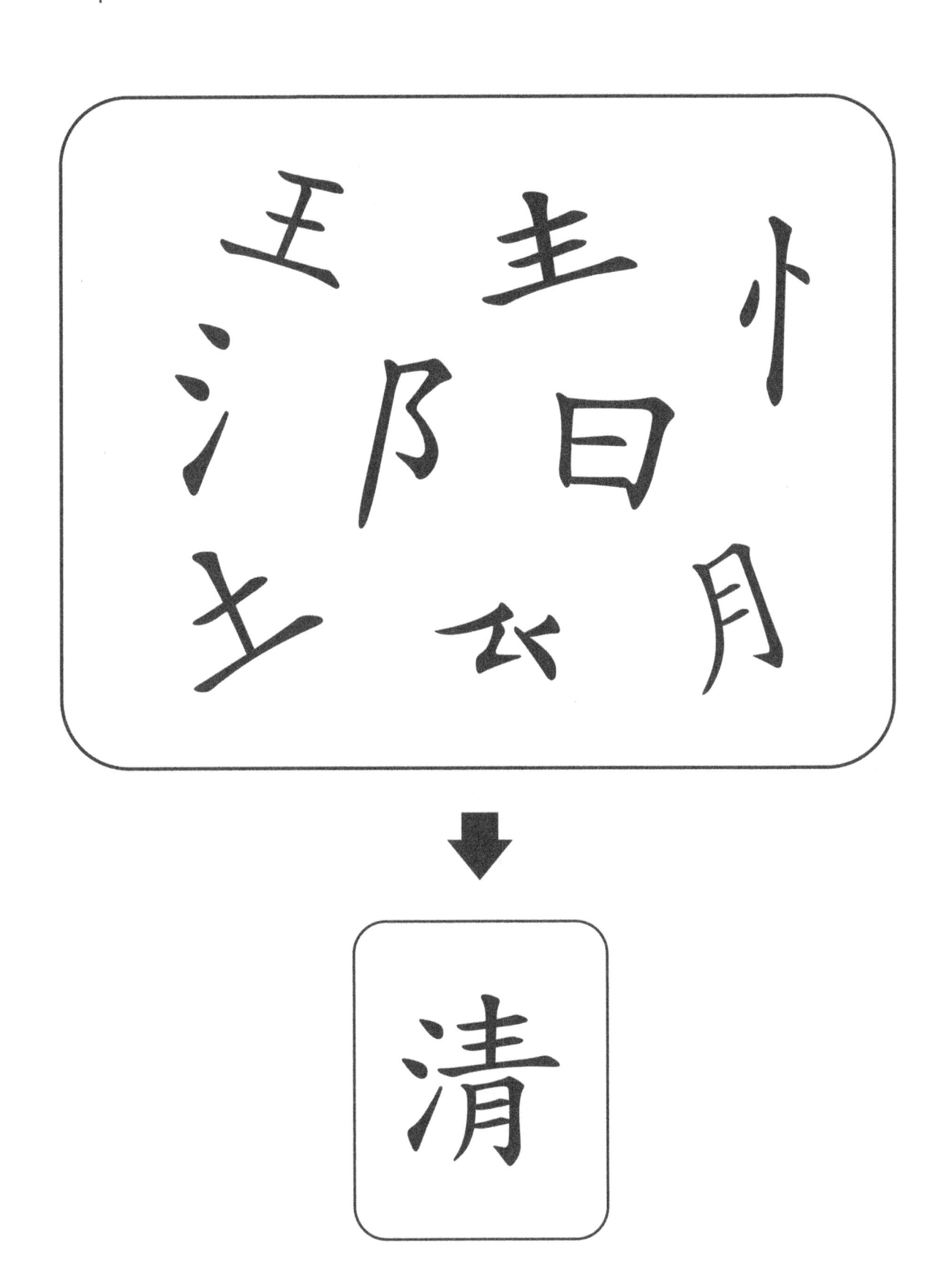

王　圭　卜
氵　阝　日
主　　ㄙ　月

清

請在與圖案相對應的句子前面打勾。
Put a checkmark in front of the phrase that best describes the picture.

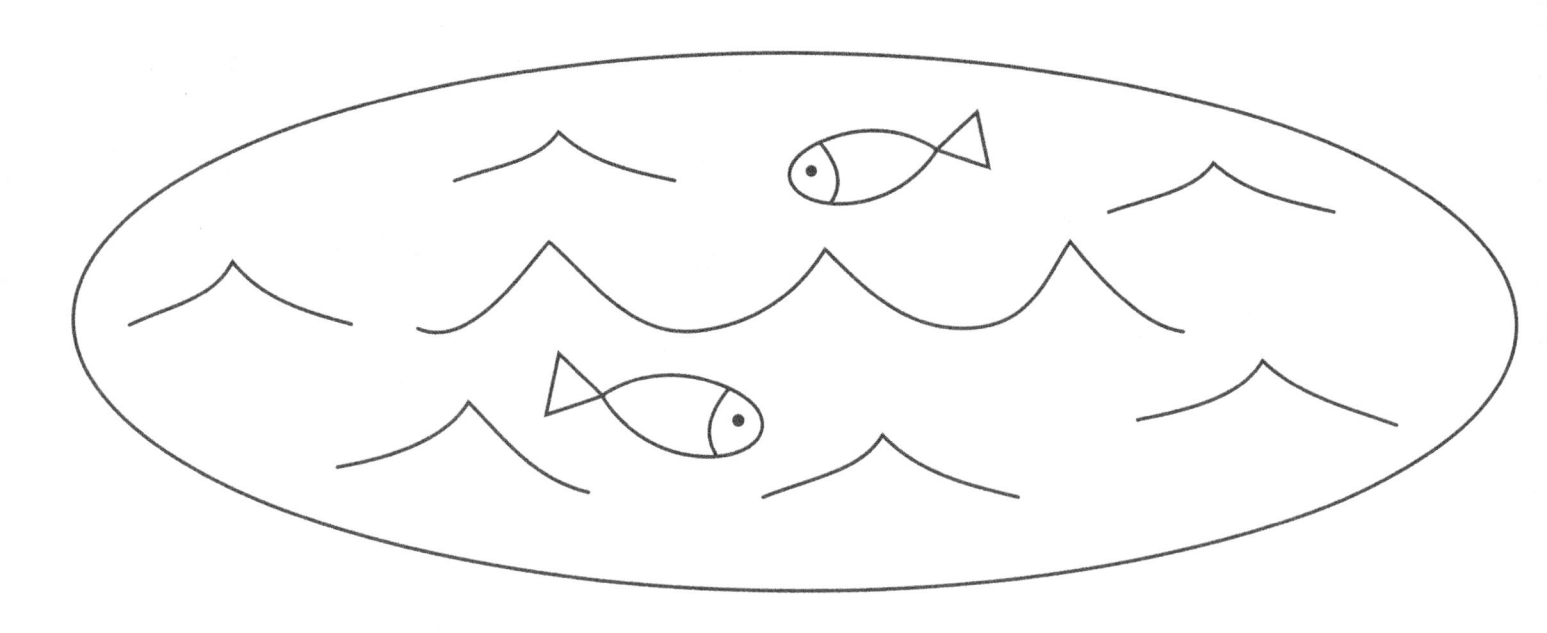

（　）水中沒有魚。

（　）魚兒和小狗一起玩。

（　）小貓想吃魚。

（　）水很清，看得見魚。

唸唸看
Read-Aloud

- 媽媽要我清理房間。
  Mom wants me to clean the room.

- 我把妹妹的衣服收到右邊，我的衣服收到左邊。
  I put away (my) younger sister's clothes to the right side, and my clothes to the left side.

- 我還把地上的灰也清理了，房間都變亮了呢。
  I also cleaned up the dust on the floor. The room even became brighter.

- 我樂於幫忙媽媽做家事，這一點都不難。
  I am happy to help Mom do chores. It is not hard at all.

- 媽媽等會兒可以安心去看電視了。
  Later, Mom can go watch television comfortably.

恭喜你完成了這一課，請回到第一頁將本課的花朵塗上顏色。
Congratulations! You have completed a lesson. Please color the flower for this lesson on page 1.

第十八課

Lesson 18 Gāi – should; ought to; must be; probably; to deserve

本書中的國字筆順是依據中華民國教育部「常用國字標準字體筆順學習網」的筆劃順序彙編。
The stroke orders of the characters in this workbook follow the stroke orders provided on the "Learning Program for Stroke Order of Frequently Used Chinese Characters" website of the Ministry of Education, R.O.C. (Taiwan).

請將下方的字格剪下來讓孩子選擇正確的字貼上。
Please cut out the characters at the bottom and paste the correct one.

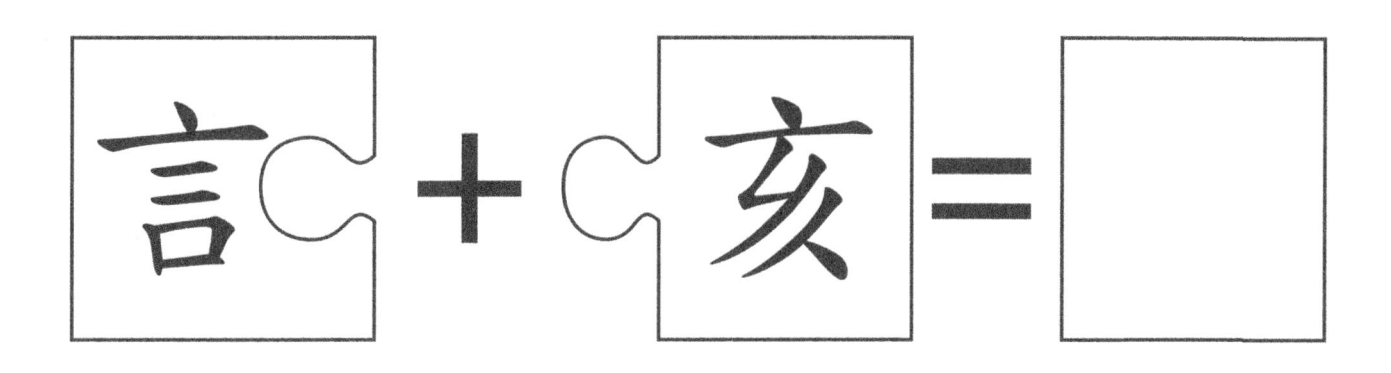

言 + 亥 = ☐

| 言 | 亥 | 該 | 孩 | 核 |

請在與圖案相對應的句子前面打勾。
Put a checkmark in front of the phrase that best describes the picture.

（　）天亮了，該起床了。
（　）時候不早了，該上學了。
（　）這麼晚了，該睡了！
（　）這麼晚了，該回家了。

唸唸看
Read-Aloud

- 我在清理花園時在土裡找到了一些黃金。
  When I was cleaning the garden, (I) found some gold in the ground.

- 我不該拿不是我的東西,不然我心會不安。
  I shouldn't take what is not mine, otherwise I will feel guilty.

- 我左右看了又看就是找不到黃金的主人。
  I looked left and right and couldn't find the owner of the gold.

- 於是我又把黃金放回土裡。
  Therefore, I put the gold back into the ground.

- 如果黃金的主人找不到黃金會心情不好的。
  If the owner of the gold can't find the gold, (he) will be in a bad mood.

恭喜你完成了這一課,請回到第一頁將本課的花朵塗上顏色。
Congratulations! You have completed a lesson. Please color the flower for this lesson on page 1.

第十九課

Lesson 19 Yīng – should; ought to; must
Yìng – to answer; to respond; to deal with

本書中的國字筆順是依據中華民國教育部「常用國字標準字體筆順學習網」的筆劃順序彙編。
The stroke orders of the characters in this workbook follow the stroke orders provided on the "Learning Program for Stroke Order of Frequently Used Chinese Characters" website of the Ministry of Education, R.O.C. (Taiwan).

圈出可以組成下面文字的部分。
Circle the parts that form the character at the bottom.

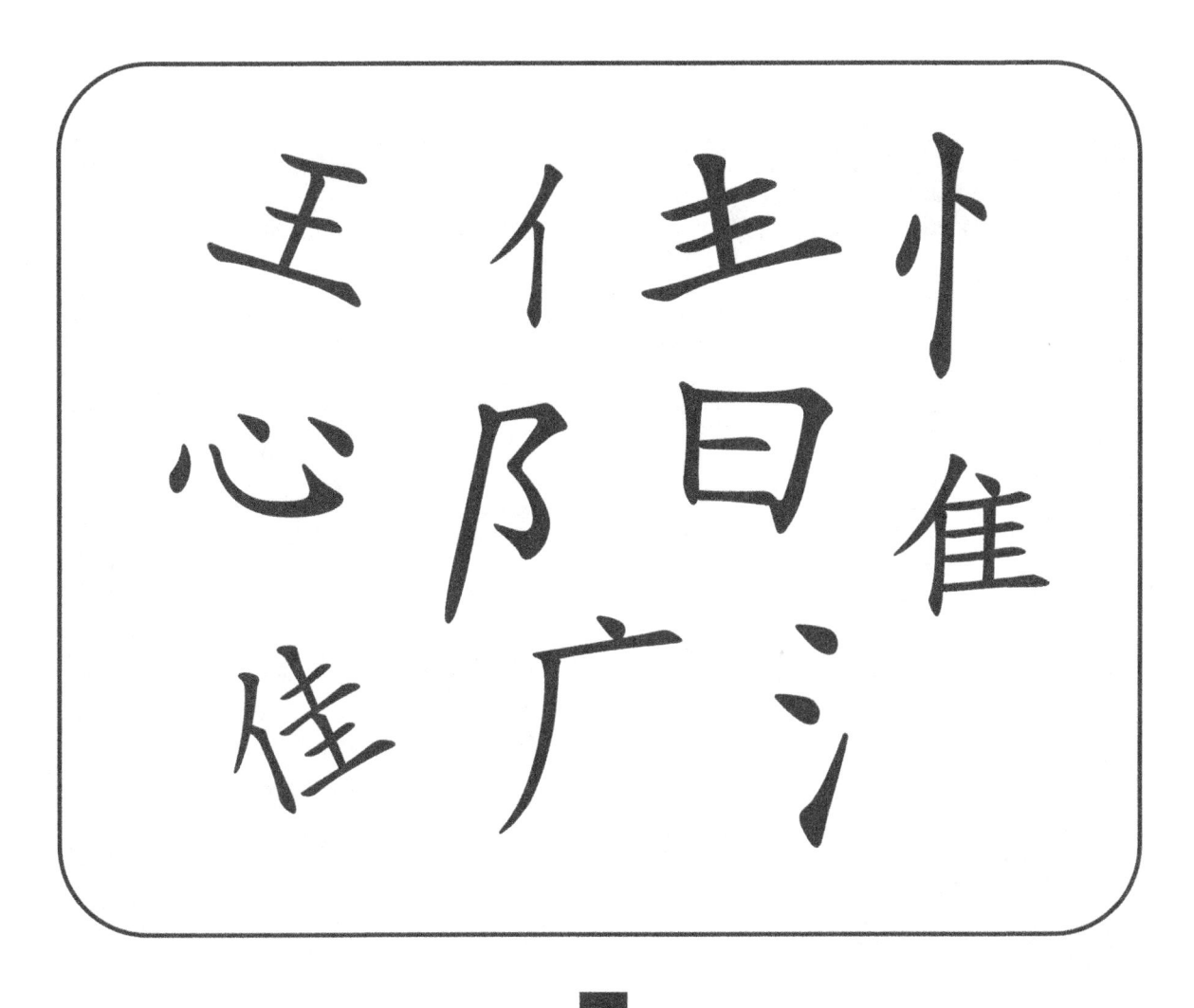

王 亻 圭 卜
　　曰　隹
心 阝 氵
　佳 广

↓

應

跟著「應」字從 ➡ 到 ★ 走出迷宮。
Follow the characters 應 from the arrow to the star to exit the maze.

唸唸看
Read-Aloud

- 明年我想要坐飛機去美國看國家隊的比賽。

  Next year I want to take the plane to the U.S.A. to watch the national team compete.

- 他們這次應該可以拿到第一名。

  They should be able to get first place this time.

- 做運動前應該先清理好場地,還要小心安全才不會拉傷。

  Before exercising, (you) should clear up the site, and also be careful not to pull a muscle.

- 像妹妹那樣不看路地左跳右跳其實很可怕。

  Jumping left and right without watching the way like (my) younger sister is very dangerous.

- 要是等一下受傷的話,她應該會哭得很傷心。

  If (she) gets hurt later, she probably will cry sadly.

恭喜你完成了這一課,請回到第一頁將本課的花朵塗上顏色。
Congratulations! You have completed a lesson. Please color the flower for this lesson on page 1.

第二十課

Lesson 20 Rù – to enter; to go into

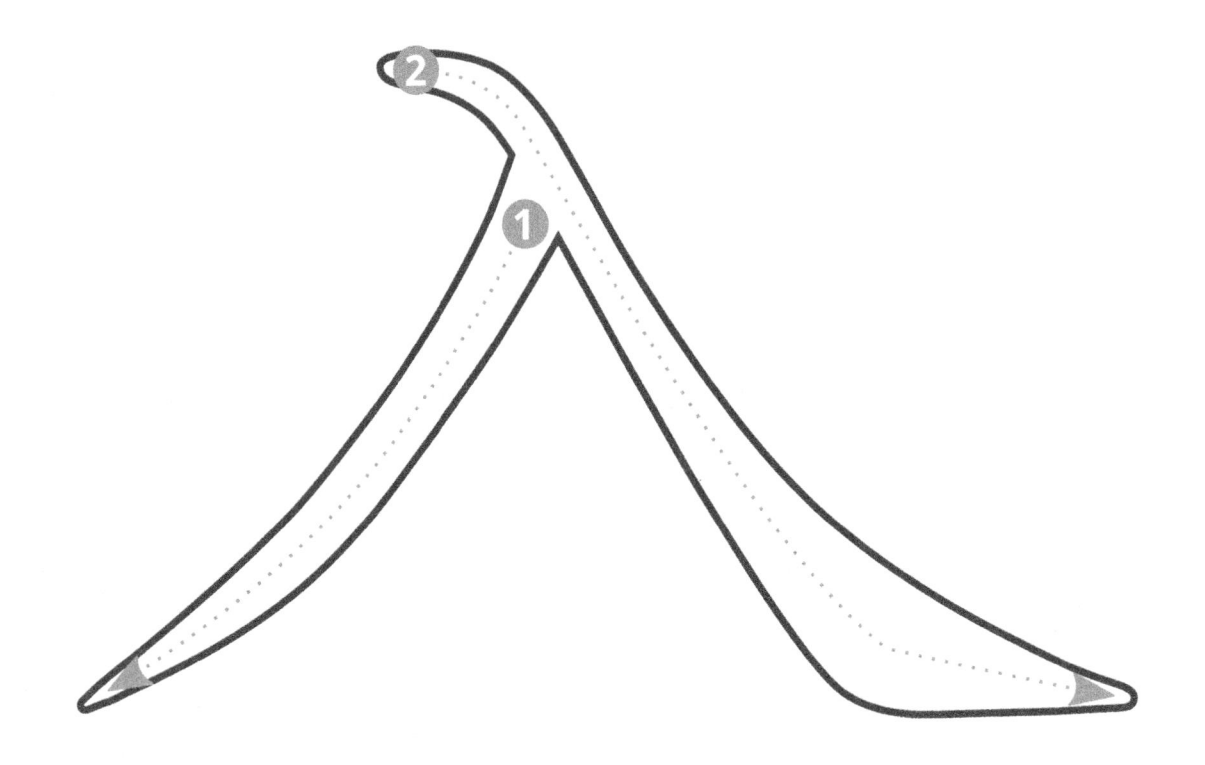

本書中的國字筆順是依據中華民國教育部「常用國字標準字體筆順學習網」的筆劃順序彙編。
The stroke orders of the characters in this workbook follow the stroke orders provided on the "Learning Program for Stroke Order of Frequently Used Chinese Characters" website of the Ministry of Education, R.O.C. (Taiwan).

請圈出可以到達螞蟻窩的入口。
Please circle the entrance that leads to the ant.

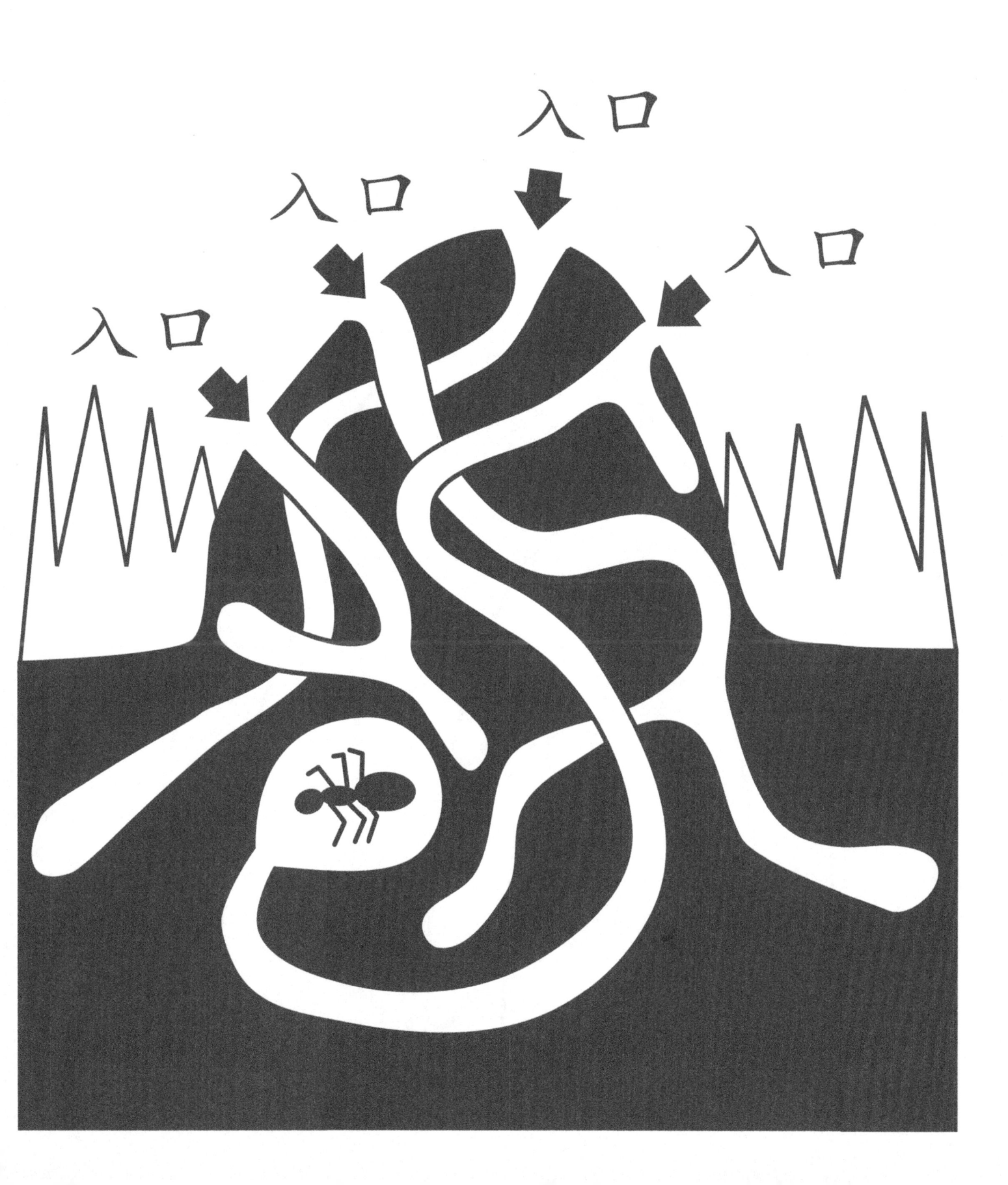

入口　入口　入口　入口

80

連連看一樣的字。
Draw a line to the matching character.

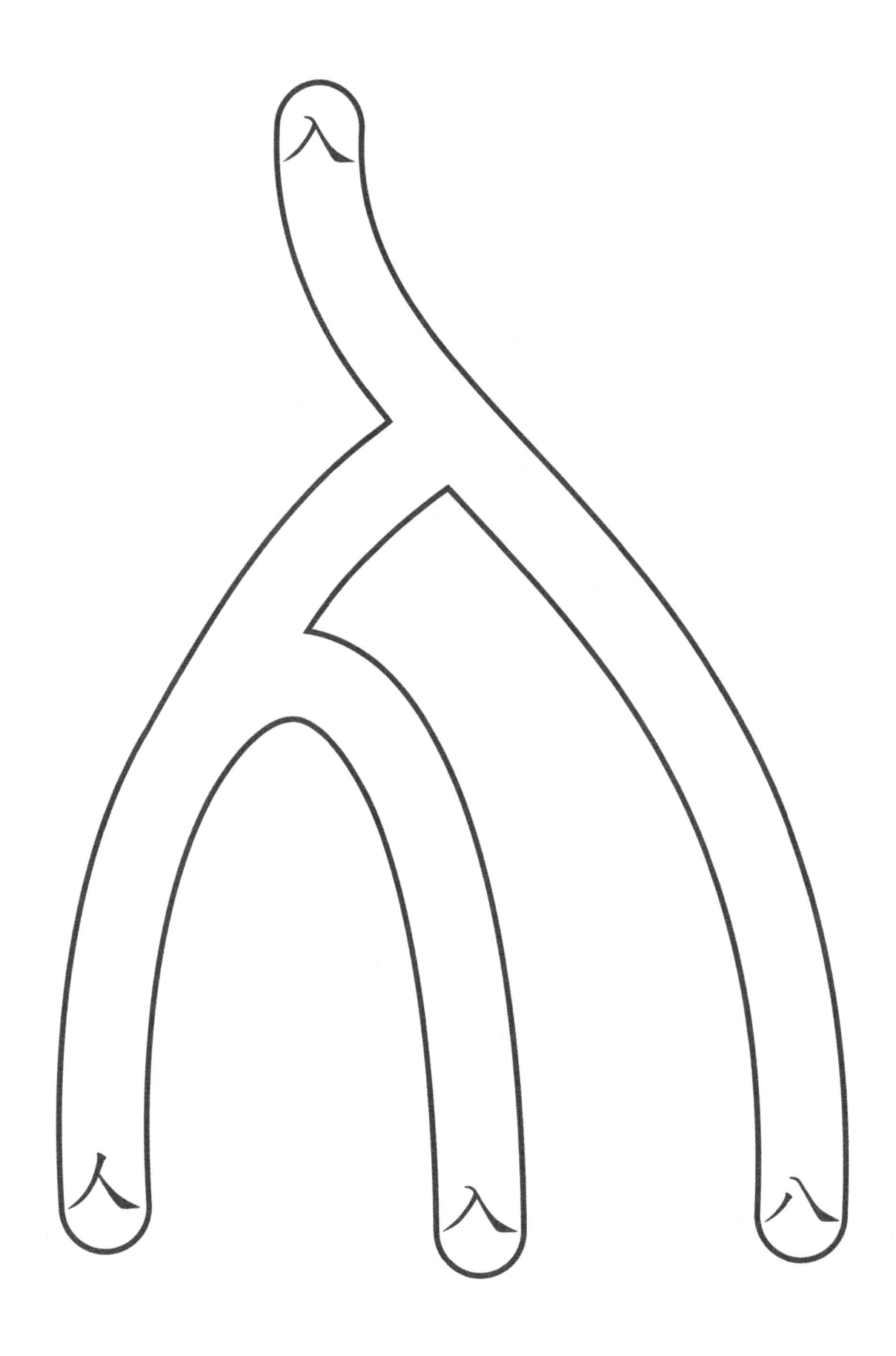

唸唸看
Read-Aloud

- 妹妹在家裡高聲唱了好幾首歌。
  (My) younger sister loudly sang many songs at home.

- 弟弟要睡覺所以媽媽叫妹妹去公園唱。
  (My) younger brother wants to sleep, therefore Mom told (my) younger sister to go to the park to sing.

- 我和妹妹去了一個新的公園，可是我們找不到入口。
  (My) younger sister and I went to a new park, but we cannot find the entrance.

- 路人和我們說入口應該就在前面，可是我們還是分不清方向。
  A passerby told us that the entrance should be at the front, but we still can't figure out the direction.

- 天已經黑了，我們還是沒有找到入口，感覺很不安全。
  It is dark already, and we still haven't found the entrance. (We) do not feel very safe.

恭喜你完成了這一課，請回到第一頁將本課的花朵塗上顏色。
Congratulations! You have completed a lesson. Please color the flower for this lesson on page 1.

第二十一課

Lesson 21 Shí – rock; stone

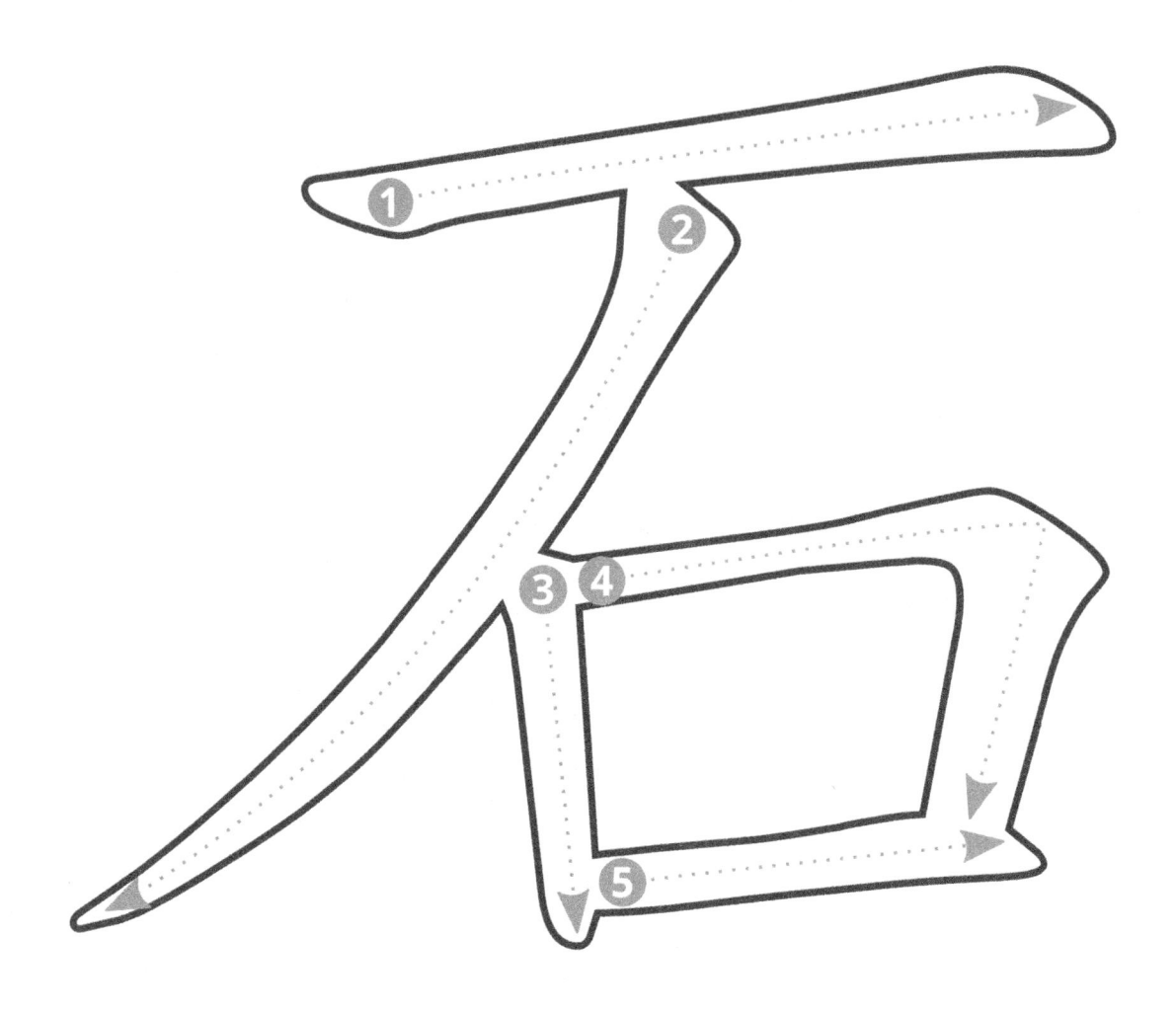

本書中的國字筆順是依據中華民國教育部「常用國字標準字體筆順學習網」的筆劃順序彙編。
The stroke orders of the characters in this workbook follow the stroke orders provided on the "Learning Program for Stroke Order of Frequently Used Chinese Characters" website of the Ministry of Education, R.O.C. (Taiwan).

「石」是象形字。
The character 石 is a pictograph.

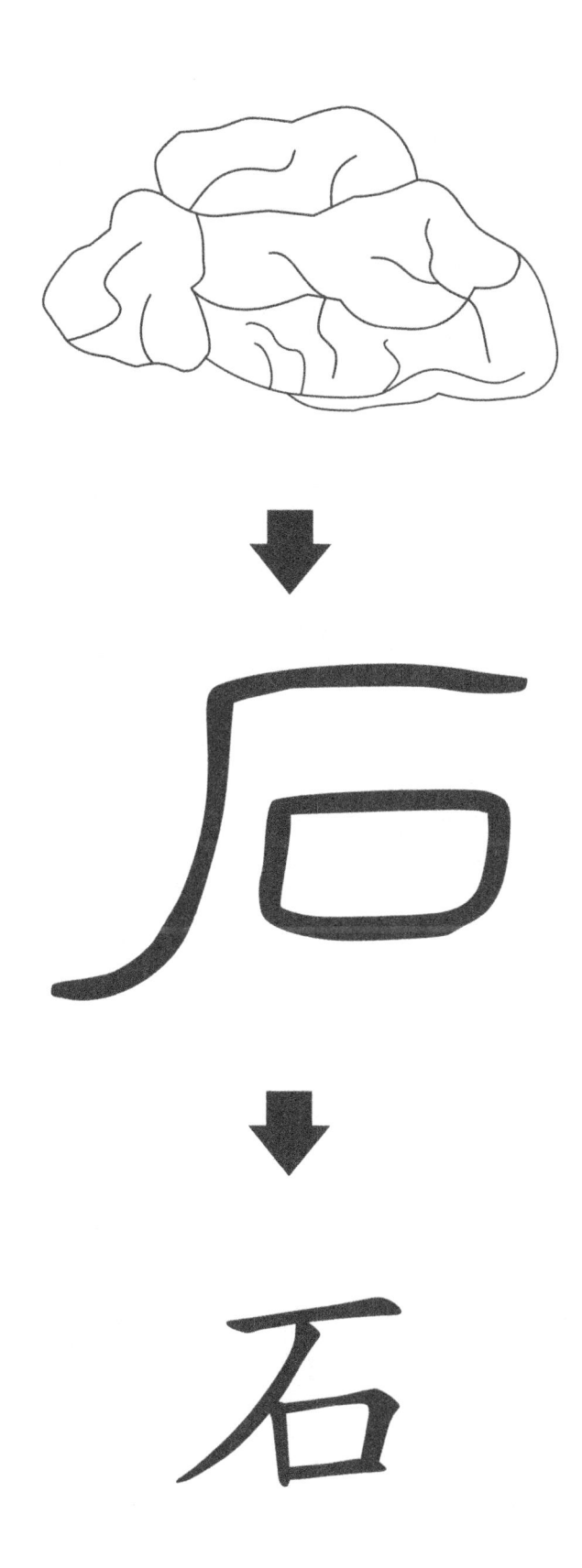

圖案中有的東西在（ ）中打勾。
Put a check next to the items that are in the picture.

( ) 房子　　( ) 水車　　( ) 鳥
( ) 太陽　　( ) 石頭　　( ) 樹
( ) 河　　　( ) 天空　　( ) 花
( ) 白雲　　( ) 草地　　( ) 豬

唸唸看
Read-Aloud

- 今天我們終於找到公園的入口了。
  Today we finally found the park's entrance.

- 我和妹妹開心地坐在公園裡說話。
  (My) younger sister and I happily sat in the park to talk.

- 我和妹妹說雲其實是清水做的。
  I told (my) younger sister that clouds are actually made of water.

- 妹妹問：「石頭是火做的嗎？」
  (My) younger sister asked, "Are rocks made of fire?"

- 我說：「石頭應該不是火做的吧，我下次去問老師。」
  I said, "Rocks shouldn't be made of fire. Next time I will ask the teacher."

恭喜你完成了這一課，請回到第一頁將本課的花朵塗上顏色。
Congratulations! You have completed a lesson. Please color the flower for this lesson on page 1.

第二十二課

Lesson 22 Jiā – to add; plus

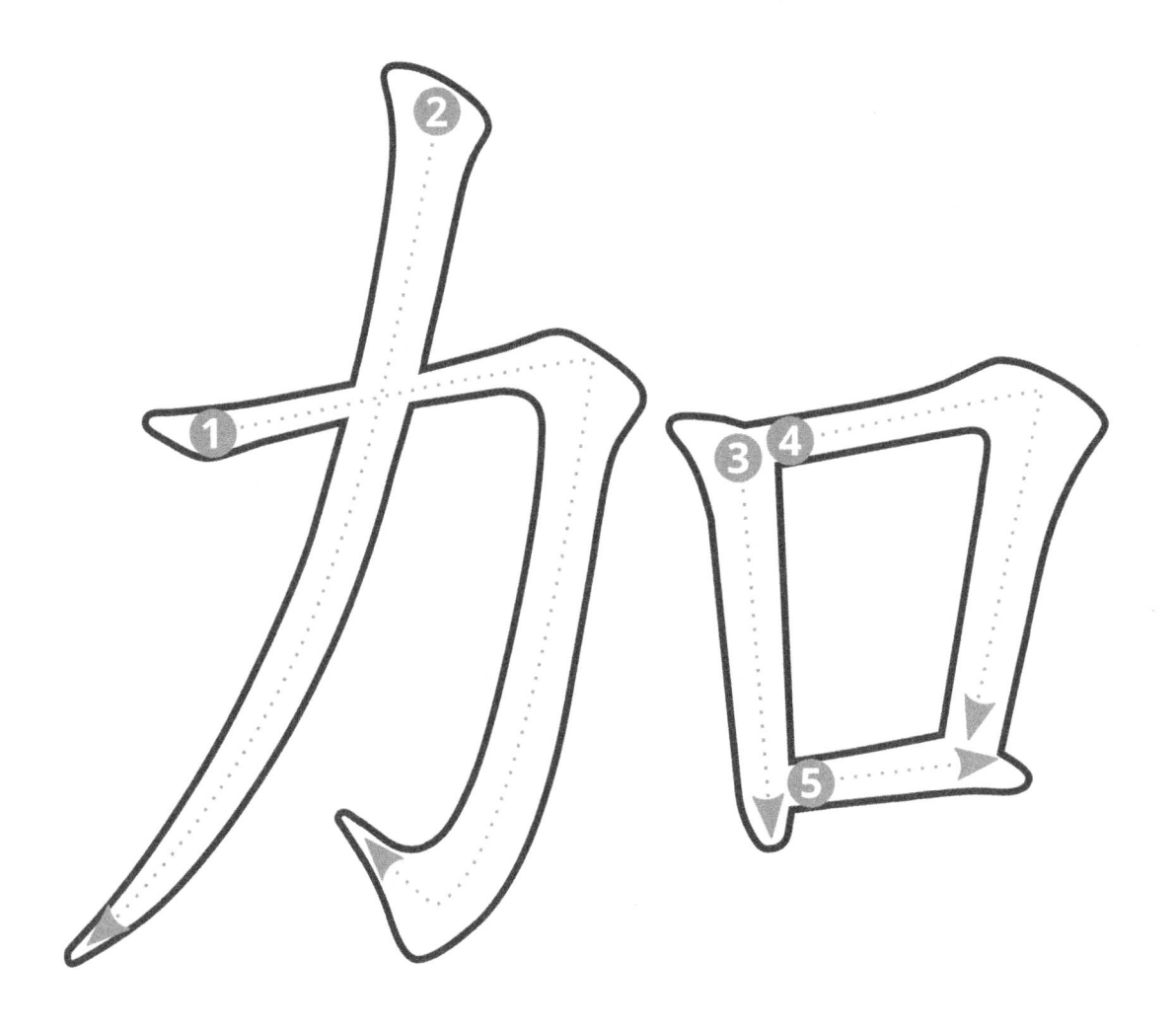

本書中的國字筆順是依據中華民國教育部「常用國字標準字體筆順學習網」的筆劃順序彙編。
The stroke orders of the characters in this workbook follow the stroke orders provided on the "Learning Program for Stroke Order of Frequently Used Chinese Characters" website of the Ministry of Education, R.O.C. (Taiwan).

請將下方的字格剪下來讓孩子選擇正確的字貼上。
Please cut out the characters at the bottom and paste the correct one.

力 + 口 = ☐

| 力 | 口 | 咖 | 另 | 加 |

請在右邊圈出正確的答案。
Please circle the correct answers on the right.

一加一　　　等於　　　二／五

二加一　　　等於　　　五／三

三加一　　　等於　　　二／四

五加一　　　等於　　　六／五

十加一　　　等於　　　九／十一

唸唸看
Read-Aloud

- 如果每一間房子都有兩個出入口，兩間房子應該有幾個出入口？

  If every house has two entrances, how many entrances should there be for two houses?

- 二加二等於四，所以會有四個出入口。

  Two plus two equals four, therefore there are four entrances.

- 小明找到了五顆紅色的石頭和五顆藍色的石頭，小明一共有幾顆石頭？

  Ming found five red rocks and five blue rocks. How many rocks does Ming have in total?

- 五加五等於十，所以小明一共有十顆石頭。

  Five plus five equals ten, therefore Ming has ten rocks in total.

- 今天老師出的數學應用題我全部都答對了。

  I answered all of the math word problems, assigned by the teacher today, correctly.

恭喜你完成了這一課，請回到第一頁將本課的花朵塗上顏色。
Congratulations! You have completed a lesson. Please color the flower for this lesson on page 1.

第二十三課

Lesson 23 Fǎ – law; method

本書中的國字筆順是依據中華民國教育部「常用國字標準字體筆順學習網」的筆劃順序彙編。
The stroke orders of the characters in this workbook follow the stroke orders provided on the "Learning Program for Stroke Order of Frequently Used Chinese Characters" website of the Ministry of Education, R.O.C. (Taiwan).

請在與圖案相對應的句子前面打勾。
Put a checkmark in front of the phrase that best describes the picture.

（　）小妹妹寫書法。

（　）小妹妹愛唱歌。

（　）小妹妹在吃東西。

（　）小妹妹在玩球。

畫出路線，連出一句話。
Connect the characters to form a sentence.

這	是	力	得	它
口	一	個	安	目
人	了	很	好	右
入	王	多	的	石
可	加	去	方	法

唸唸看
Read-Aloud

- 我在學校學加法。
  I learn addition at school.

- 我會用小石子來算加法。
  I know how to use little pebbles to calculate addition (problems).

- 我覺得這個方法應該很好用。
  I think this method should be very useful.

- 公園入口的地方有很多小石子。
  There are many small pebbles at the park's entrance.

- 我都是從那裡拿的。
  I got them all from there.

恭喜你完成了這一課,請回到第一頁將本課的花朵塗上顏色。
Congratulations! You have completed a lesson. Please color the flower for this lesson on page 1.

第二十四課
Lesson 24 Ràng – to yield; to permit

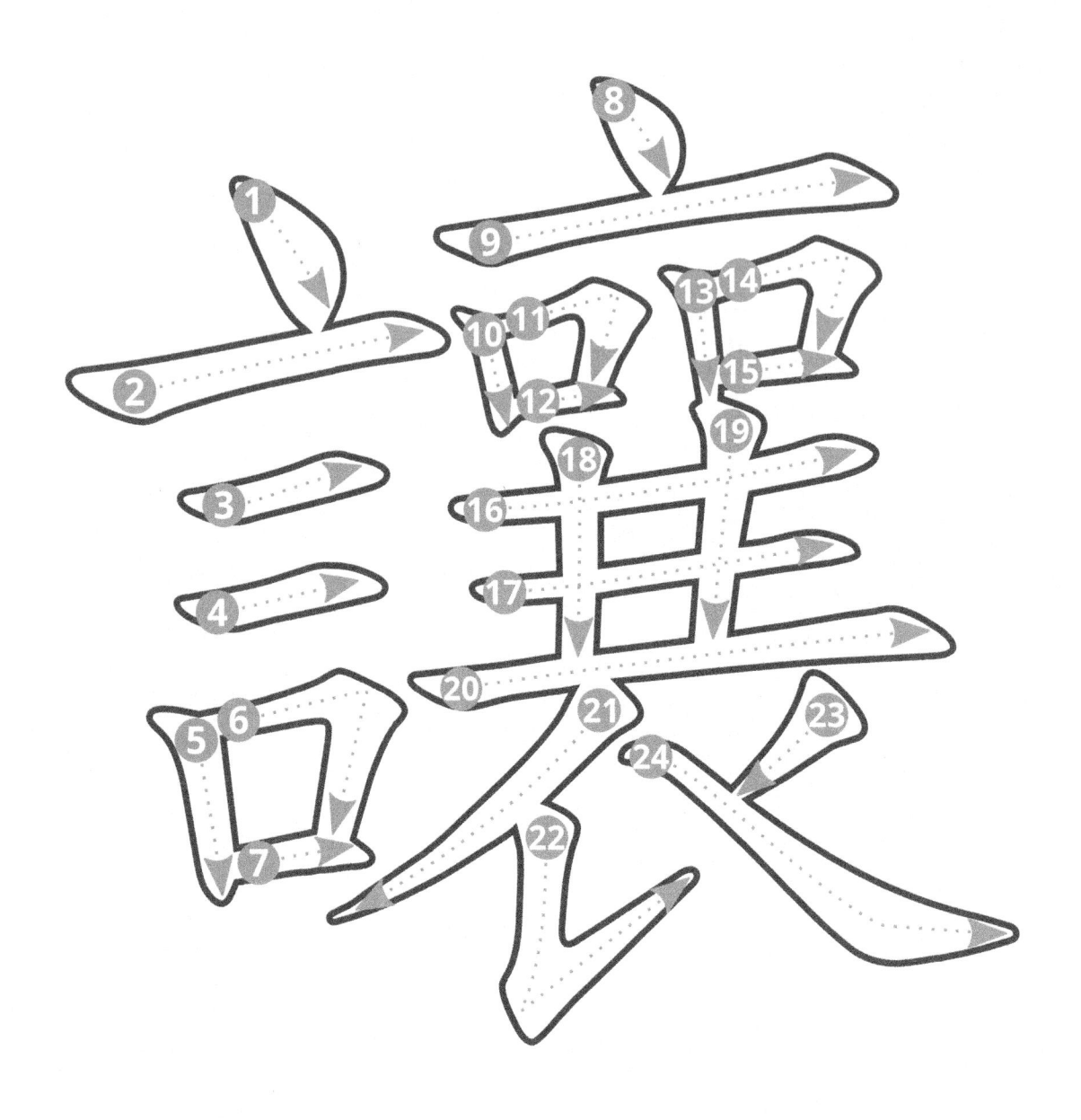

本書中的國字筆順是依據中華民國教育部「常用國字標準字體筆順學習網」的筆劃順序彙編。
The stroke orders of the characters in this workbook follow the stroke orders provided on the "Learning Program for Stroke Order of Frequently Used Chinese Characters" website of the Ministry of Education, R.O.C. (Taiwan).

請把救護車連到讓路標誌。
Please connect the ambulance to the yield sign.

96

請將有「讓」字的梨著色。
Please color the pears with the character 讓.

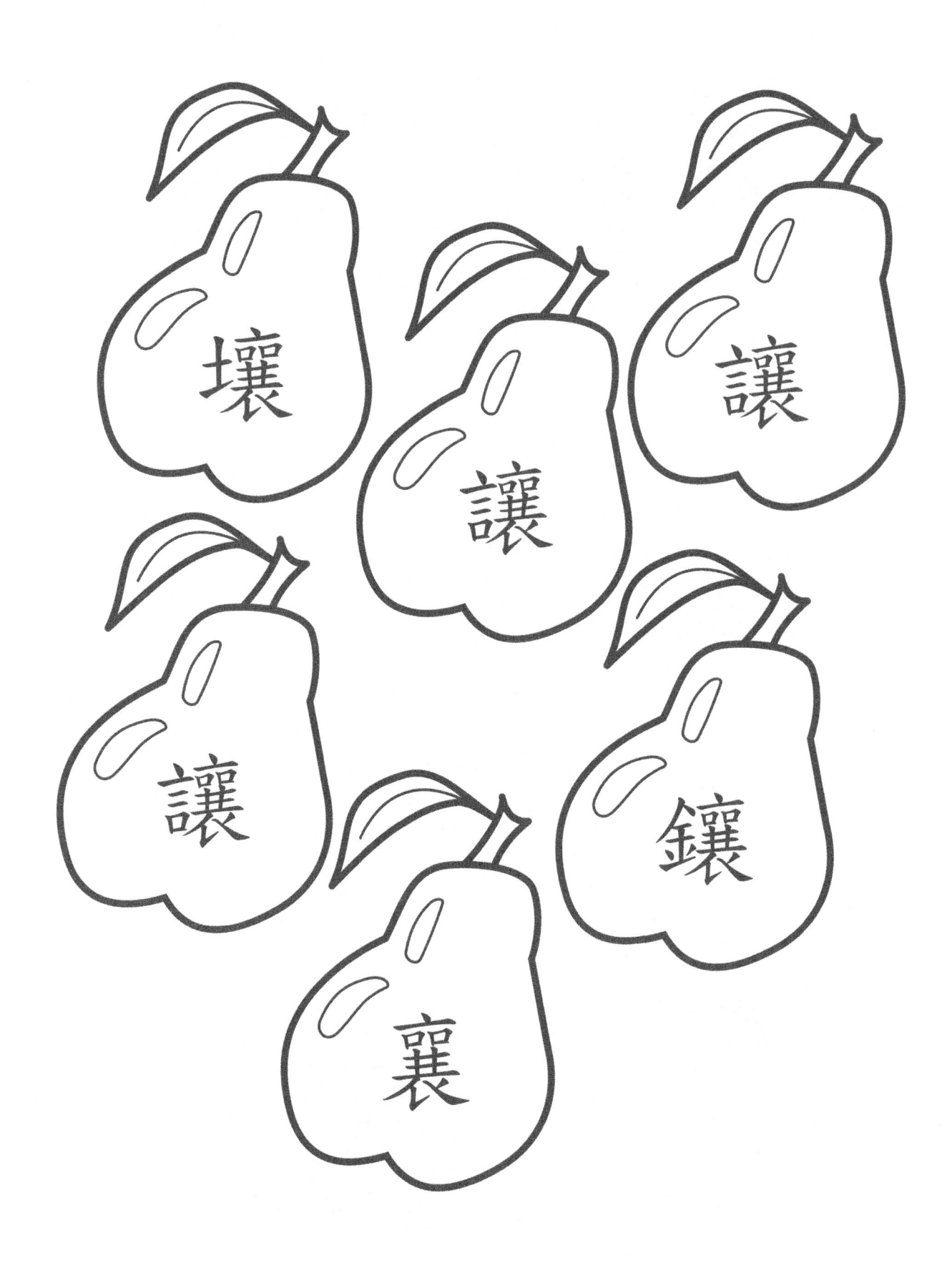

壞　讓　讓　讓　鑲　襄

唸唸看
Read-Aloud

- 電影院不讓我們帶自己的食物進入。
The movie theater doesn't let us bring our own food in.

- 我問電影院的人可不可以讓我帶學加法的小石子進去。
I ask the people working at the movie theater (if they) will let me bring the little pebbles I use for learning math in.

- 他們說沒問題，但是要記得帶回家。
They say there is no problem, but (I) need to remember to bring it home.

- 我也說沒問題。
I also say no problem.

恭喜你完成了這一課，請回到第一頁將本課的花朵塗上顏色。
Congratulations! You have completed a lesson. Please color the flower for this lesson on page 1.

第二十五課

Lesson 25 Xǐ – to like; to be happy

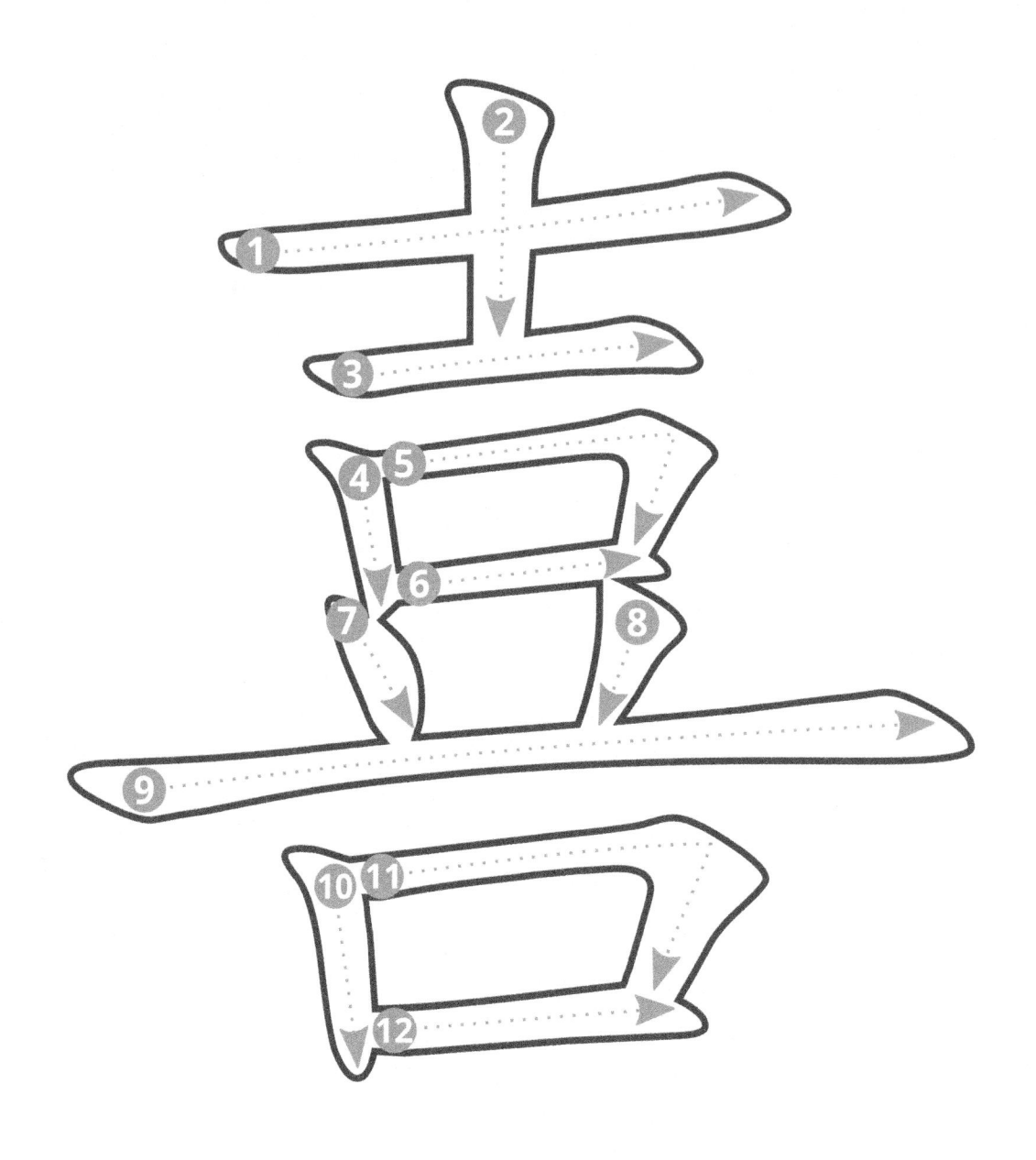

本書中的國字筆順是依據中華民國教育部「常用國字標準字體筆順學習網」的筆劃順序彙編。
The stroke orders of the characters in this workbook follow the stroke orders provided on the "Learning Program for Stroke Order of Frequently Used Chinese Characters" website of the Ministry of Education, R.O.C. (Taiwan).

跟著「喜」字從 ➡ 到 ★ 走出迷宮。
Follow the characters 喜 from the arrow to the star to exit the maze.

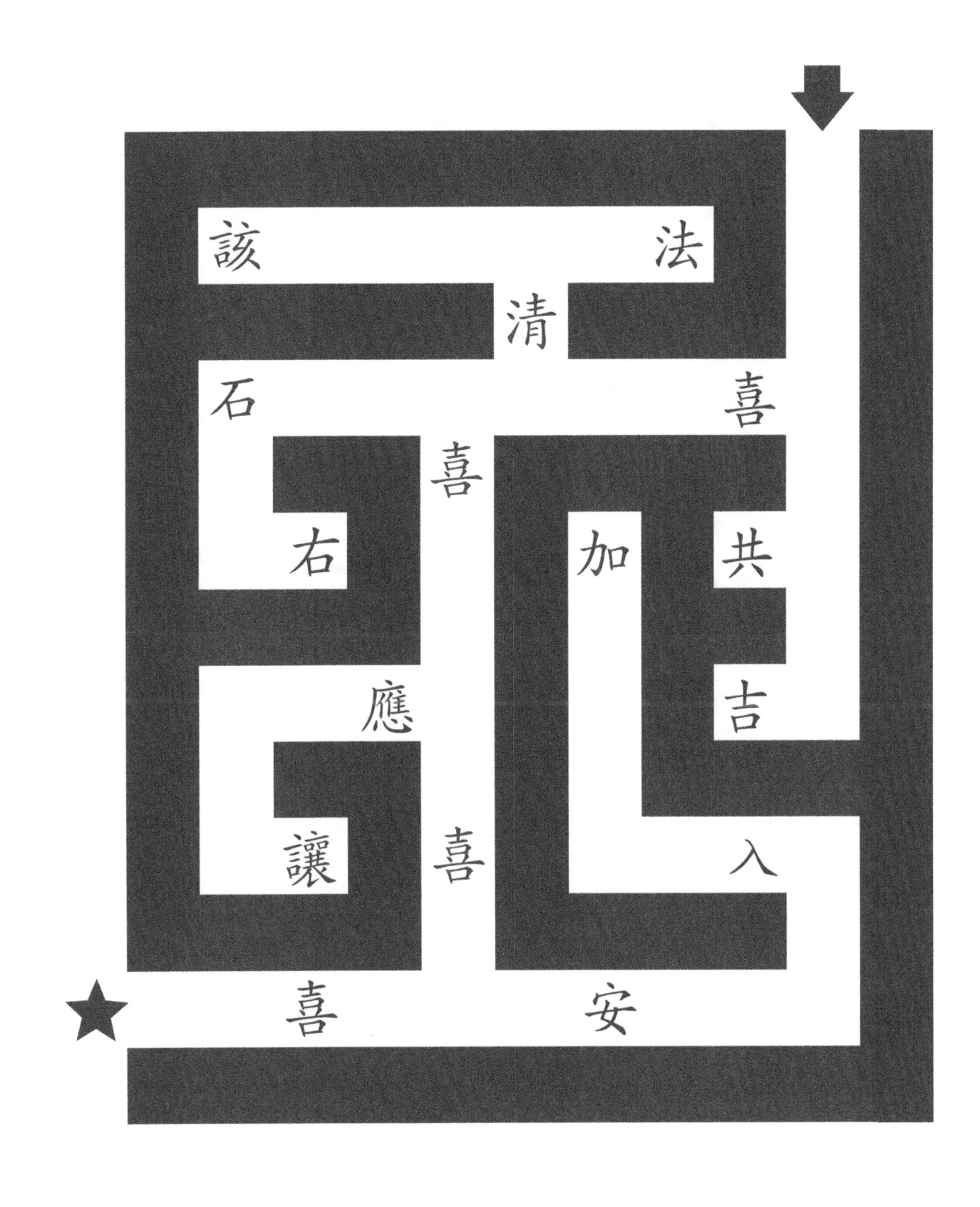

100

圈出可以組成下面文字的部分。
Circle the parts that form the character at the bottom.

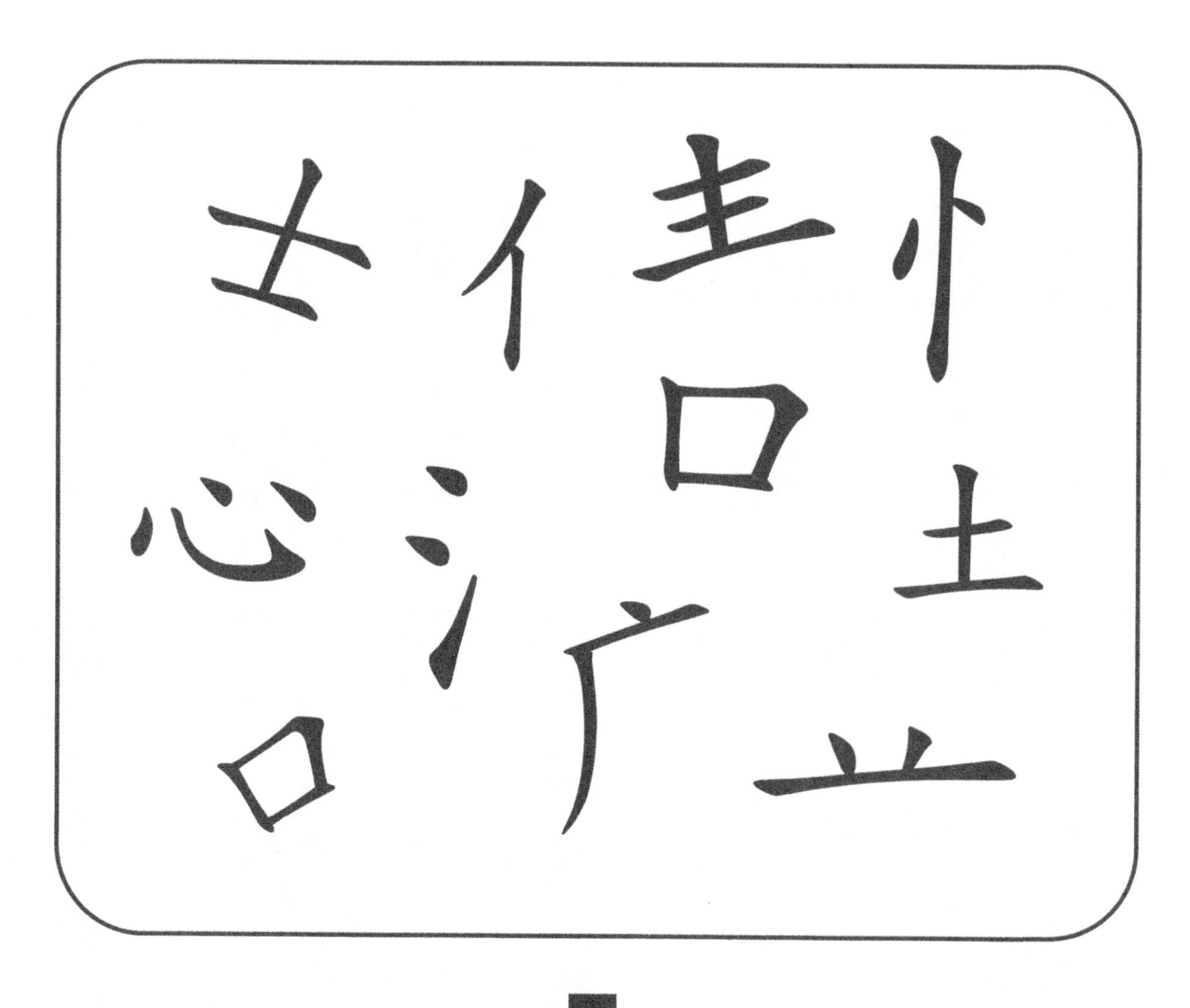

士　亻　吉　卜
心　口　氵　土
　　　口　广　丷

↓

喜

唸唸看
Read-Aloud

- 我最喜愛的老師是數學老師。
  My favorite teacher is the math teacher.

- 我最喜愛的課是數學課。
  My favorite class is math class.

- 數學老師讓我們用小石頭學加法。
  The math teacher lets us use small pebbles to do addition.

- 老師要我們用石頭算一算八隻豬一共有幾隻耳朵。
  The teacher wants us to use small pebbles to calculate how many ears eight pigs have in total.

- 我覺得用這個方法真好玩。
  I think using this method is really fun.

恭喜你完成了這一課，請回到第一頁將本課的花朵塗上顏色。
Congratulations! You have completed a lesson. Please color the flower for this lesson on page 1.

獎狀
Certificate of Achievement

恭喜

Congratulations to

_____

完成趣味識字第十五冊。
特發此狀以資鼓勵！

for completing Fun with Chinese Workbook 15.

_____   _____
簽名 Signature   日期 Date

Made in the USA
Las Vegas, NV
21 April 2025